FEATURES

SPRING 2023 • NUMBER 35

D1810794

Plough

Plough

ANOTHER LIFE IS POSSIBLE

EDITOR: Peter Mommsen
SENIOR EDITORS: Shana Goodwin, Maria Hine, Maureen Swinger, Sam Hine, Susannah Black Roberts
EDITOR-AT-LARGE: Caitrin Keiper
BOOKS AND CULTURE EDITOR: Joy Marie Clarkson
POETRY EDITOR: A M Juster
DESIGNERS: Rosalind Stevenson, Miriam Burleson
CREATIVE DIRECTOR: Clare Stober
COPY EDITORS: Wilma Mommsen, Priscilla Jensen
FACT CHECKER: Suzanne Quinta
MARKETING DIRECTOR: Trevor Wiser
UK EDITION: Ian Barth
CONTRIBUTING EDITORS: Leah Libresco Sargeant, Brandon McGinley, Jake Meador
FOUNDING EDITOR: Eberhard Arnold (1883–1935)

Plough Quarterly No 35: Pain and Passion
Published by Plough Publishing House, ISBN 978-0-87486-004-7
Copyright © 2023 by Plough Publishing House. All rights reserved.

EDITORIAL OFFICE
United Kingdom
Brightling Road
Robertsbridge
TN32 5DR
T: +44(0)1580.883.344

United States
151 Bowne Drive
Walden, NY 12586, USA
T: +1.845.572.3455
info@plough.com

SUBSCRIBER SERVICES
Plough Quarterly
Unit 6, The Enterprise Centre
Kelvin Lane, Crawley RH10 9PE
T:0800.018.0799
plough@subscriptionhelpline.co.uk

Australia
4188 Gwydir Highway
Elsmore, NSW
2360 Australia
T: +61(0)2.6723.2213

Plough Quarterly (ISSN 9780874860047) is published quarterly by Plough Publishing House, Brightling Road, Robertsbridge TN32 5DR..
Individual subscription £24/ €28 / $36 per year.
Subscribers outside of the United States and Canada pay in British pounds or euros.
Periodicals postage paid at Walden, NY 12586, USA, and at additional mailing offices.
POSTMASTER: Send address changes to
Plough Quarterly, Unit 6, The Enterprise Center, Kelvin Lane, Crawley RH10 9PE

Front cover: Daniel Bonnell, *Pieta Meditation #1*, oil on canvas, 2019. Used by permission.
Inside front cover: Edvard Munch, *Spring Ploughing*, oil on canvas, 1916. Public domain.
Back cover: Michelangelo Buonarroti, *Madonna della Pietà*, Carrara marble sculpture, 1498–1499 (detail). Public domain.

ABOUT THE COVER

Michelangelo Buonarroti's *Pietà* is a powerful study in pain – both the physical pain Christ passed through, and the soul's pain evident in Mary's posture. Our front cover artwork is a meditation on the *Pietà* by contemporary artist Daniel Bonnell.

LETTERS

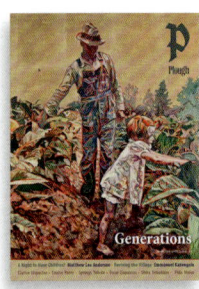

Readers respond to *Plough*'s Winter 2023 issue, 'Generations'. Send letters to *letters@plough.com*.

THE HOSPITALITY OF ADOPTION

On Wendy Kiyomi's 'The Stranger in My House': Years ago, my wife and I adopted an 11-year-old son, Brian. We had attended all of the adoption/foster training classes and met with numerous counsellors, as well as others who had adopted. Our minds, hearts and prayers were like those you express so well. Brian had suffered unbelievable neglect, trauma, abuse and loss in his early childhood. He came to us 'on trial' from a foster home, one of four he had stayed with over the past year. When we agreed to adopt him, he arrived carrying a big black plastic rubbish bag that held all his personal belongings. We later learned it was known as the 'foster suitcase'.

It has now been over two decades since his arrival and his ugly departure when he turned 17 and left out of the front door, not looking back. Since his departure, his life and ours have been in such turmoil it would take a book to write it all. Many friends and family are still hesitant to ask about him, but when they do, we have learned to say: 'He is God's child, and the story is still not over.' Please pray for those of us who have opened our homes and our hearts to these children and pray for these children, who suffered and continue to suffer such pain, sorrow and grief.

Bill Chadwick, Louisa, Virginia USA

I was so grateful to read this wise, beautiful counsel as I'm in the midst of an inner struggle about how to best serve my adult, informally adopted child who became more distant than ever after I needed to cut off financial support.

Frankly, it makes me wonder in my darkest hours if our relationship has been based upon transactions of goods and if it would be better to exit completely from giving gifts. I know the pain distorts my deeper understanding, and your article restored it.

As humans we do want to see results; we want to see the children we've poured [love] into 'win' against evil, and we want to feel loved, appreciated, noticed; we want some confirmation from them as a message from God that our 'investment' was well spent.

On my good days I know these are false idols, but at times the pain can bring the temptation for resentment and self-pity. I am grateful that you point us back to the fact that none of this is biblical, but that the act of such deep and vulnerable hospitality surely is.

Megan L Prather, Madison, Wisconsin USA

THE LONGING FOR CHILDREN

On Matthew Lee Anderson's 'Is There a Right to Have Children?': Thank you for a rare, thoughtful approach to this difficult topic. If I may offer an additional thought worth consideration, it would be fostering and adoption. It seems remiss to not include it in this discussion. As someone who works with orphaned and vulnerable children in Southeast Asia, I can testify that there is a tremendous need for foster and adoptive

parents. IVF seems connected to our belief that we will love biological children more than foster or adopted children. At the risk of oversimplifying, no family need be without children. But we must be open to other alternatives than having a biological child. Perhaps a couple's inability to have a biological child is God's way of meeting two needs at once: the need of a child for parents, and the need of parents for a child. Another heavy cost of IVF might be the countless children left without families, who otherwise may have been adopted. May we have sympathy both for the grief of childless parents and for the grief of parentless children. It can be powerful to reframe the question. What if childlessness is not a problem, but an opportunity? What if childlessness, like the man who was born blind (John 9), is not a punishment or because of their sin, but that the glory of God might be displayed in their lives? And what greater display of God's glory than an orphan finding a family, and in so doing meeting the deep longings of others to be parents?

Matthew Pound, Chiang Mai, Thailand

I really appreciate the gentle and thoughtful approach this essay takes. I haven't seen anything quite like it – it goes squarely against the rights-based culture we live in and questions the belief that there is a technological solution to everything.

But I object to *That Hideous Strength* as a model for a better approach. While I also love the Dimbles, it is Lewis's misogyny which is hideous – I can no longer read most of his work. That last scene, where Jane sees her husband's clothes flung over the window and realises she's got work to do is too much to accept. I'm sure the author could find a better example in literature...or is that asking too much? In real life, I know many people who have accepted tragedy with courage and grace.

Jo Chopra McGowan, Dehradun, India

THE HOPE WE TEACH

On Louise Perry's 'Fear of a Human Planet': Agree 100%. The future belongs to those who hope. A quote that should be shouted from the mountaintops. It should also be mentioned that for better or worse, those who are choosing not to have children are those who have the best chance of raising children to help solve the world's problems.

It is a travesty that schools and society at large are teaching our kids to be hopeless, a significant factor in the mental health crisis. Instead we should be teaching kids skills and perspectives that are forward-looking and solution-finding, both helping to better our global problems while also teaching agency and responsibility to young people (which increases resilience).

Shannon Huffman Polson,
Villard de Lans, France

LEARNING FROM PAST GENERATIONS

On Peter Mommsen's 'Yearning for Roots': In less than a year's time I lost both of my grandfathers. To grieve their passing was strange. Here were two men who inspired me greatly and indeed in no small way fashioned me into who I am today, yet I knew so little about their lives outside of the brief 20-odd-year window in which

I'd encountered them. Of course, I'd heard some anecdotes of their youth and young manhood – of adventures and misadventures, mostly. I had a general awareness of the hardships they overcame. But I had never really taken time to *learn about* my grandfathers as people. It wasn't until my brother and I were given the opportunity to write the obituary of my most recently deceased grandfather that I felt some greater sense of intimacy to his life (and what a rich life he'd had!).

Now, working at a long-term convalescent centre for the elderly, I wonder what stories the residents here carry – which maybe they've never told, or been asked to tell. My position allows me to connect with the ancestors of others, while I've largely missed the opportunity to connect with my own.

Connor Brown, Wheaton, Illinois USA

I agree that we do a disservice to ourselves and to others when we think we have nothing to learn from previous generations, and that they are somehow of less value than our younger generations. Mommsen seems to put a lot of the responsibility for this disinterest on the self-absorption of the young. But I see a bigger cause for this disregard: broken families. My father left when I was a toddler, and I have no memories of him. He's made no effort to keep in contact with me. He is a complete stranger. Consequently, I have no interest in discovering who he is or where he came from because he has no interest in me. If young people are failing in their duty to care for the elderly, it may be because the elderly have failed in their duty to the

young. There are entire branches of trees that have been broken off by parents, and I do not think it is children's responsibility to repair that damage.

Dalana Quintana, Tacoma, Washington USA

LOVE, PAIN AND HEALING

On Terence Sweeney's 'My Father Left Me Paperclip': This one touched a nerve. My reaction is complicated. My son and I are estranged – not my choice. His mother and I divorced decades ago when he was around six. I moved away for a job but tried to stay in touch with letters, calls, gifts, visits. She and her family were very effective at blocking and rebuffing my efforts. The story he has heard about me,

ABOUT US

Plough is published by the Bruderhof, an Anabaptist Christian community of families and singles. Members of the Bruderhof are committed to a way of radical discipleship in the spirit of the Sermon on the Mount. Inspired by the first church in Jerusalem (Acts 2 and 4), they renounce private property and share everything in common, seeking to live a life of nonviolence, justice and service to others. There are 29 Bruderhof settlements in the United States, England, Germany, Australia, Paraguay, South Korea and Austria, with around 3,000 people in all. To learn more or arrange a visit, see the community's website at *bruderhof.com*.

Plough features original stories, ideas and culture to inspire faith and action. Starting from the conviction that the teachings and example of Jesus can transform and renew our world, we aim to apply them to all aspects of life, seeking common ground with all people of goodwill regardless of creed. The goal of *Plough* is to build a living network of readers, contributors and practitioners so that, as we read in Hebrews, we may 'spur one another on towards love and good deeds'.

Plough includes contributions that we believe are worthy of our readers' consideration, whether or not we fully agree with them. Views expressed by contributors are their own and do not necessarily reflect the editorial position of *Plough* or of the Bruderhof communities.

from bits and pieces I've gleaned over the years, is nowhere near accurate. So, who I am and who I am to him are parted by a gaping gulf of misrepresentation and forced absence. I saw him at his high school graduation and then, briefly, a couple of years later. Since then he's married and has three kids. I've not met my daughter-in-law or my grandchildren. When his first child was born, my wife and I visited the town where he lives. We tried to see him and meet his family and deliver a baby gift. Again, we were rebuffed and warned in no uncertain terms to stay away, and then he severed all communication. On holidays and special occasions I text him, but he never responds. I've tried sending cards and letters but am not sure of his current address. Every day I wonder why my son so adamantly ignores me, is so ferocious in his withholding of himself. I may never know. I'm sad for Terence and what he endured and endures. I'm sad for all the fathers and sons who keep themselves from each other. I pray reconciliation and healing for us all.

Stephen R Clark,
Lansdale, Pennsylvania USA

POETS IN THIS ISSUE

Julia Nemirovskaya was born in Moscow, immigrated to the United States in 1991 and teaches Russian literature and culture at the University of Oregon. She has published three collections of poems – *Moia knizhechka* (*My Little Book*, 1998), *Vtoraia knizhechka* (*Second Little Book*, 2014) and *Slyshnee* (*More Audible*, 2021) – as well as the novel *Lis* (2017). English translations of her poems have appeared in *Washington Square Review*, *Exchanges*, *Asymptote* and other journals. She is the editor of *Disbelief: 100 Russian Anti-War Poems* (Smokestack Books, 2023).

Her poem, 'Winter', appears on page 49.

Boris Dralyuk is the author of *My Hollywood and Other Poems* (Paul Dry Books, 2022) and the translator of Isaac Babel, Andrey Kurkov, Maxim Osipov and other authors. His poems, translations and criticism have appeared in *New York Review of Books*, the *Times Literary Supplement*, the *New Yorker* and elsewhere. Formerly editor-in-chief of the *Los Angeles Review of Books*, he is currently an Associate Professor of English and Creative Writing at the University of Tulsa, Oklahoma. He is the translator of Julia Nemirovskaya's poem, 'Winter', on page 49.

Sofia M Starnes, a former Virginia Poet Laureate, is the author of six poetry collections, most recently *The Consequence of Moonlight* (Paraclete Press, 2018). Her work has appeared widely in such journals as *Poetry*, *Notre Dame Review*, *First Things*, *Bellevue Literary Review*, *Hayden's Ferry* and the Best of the Decade edition of the *Hawai'i Pacific Review*. Her poem, 'Zeal', appears on page 37.

Transforming Food

In northeast England, a small band of skip divers has become a driving force for food rescue and redistribution.

Mim Skinner

The REfUSE van which weaves webs around the highways of northeast England was collectively funded by 315 people.

They gave amounts ranging from 50-pence pieces to four-digit sums until the great day when we could finally drive it off the car park and park it next to its newly installed electric charger. Each month it intercepts around 13 tons of in-date food, otherwise destined for the skip, from retailers and food manufacturers. Then the food can make its way towards dinner tables through our café, restaurant, school projects, 'pay what you can' shelves and delivery boxes.

When we first started gathering food and people, those road webs were spun by our feet and a sagging green 2004 Golf. Before we had a 5,000-square-foot, temperature-controlled warehouse, we had a lounge crammed with boxes and piled high with pumpkins. Before we had partnership agreements with large retail firms, we walked to and from any produce sellers we could find and hoisted one another into supermarket skips after dark.

Our ecumenical Christian community hosts emergency guests and open-house meals, so this was just how we shopped. And as we learned more about the climate impact of food waste, the exercise took on greater urgency. We started out serving from our kitchen table, then in borrowed church halls and borrowed empty shops.

Though the quantities have changed, the food has always been transformed by people. It's an ugly-duckling moment: many hands from many cultures, with varying years of experience, take this landfill-bound plenitude and turn it into delicious shared meals.

We serve pumpkin soup in November and mince pies in January. The vegetables might be chopped by Ronnie, who trained as a chef after being trafficked to the United Kingdom. She put herself through cooking school before she had a fixed abode. Those same veggies might be roasted by Maz, who came to the café to fill the void of sudden widowhood and served up by Sarah, who came to gain confidence and cooking skills to use back home for her two children. She's a paid employee now, working as assistant café manager and running food workshops in schools.

There's Tattoo Dave, our caretaker, who has stayed on for years after a probation-mandated community service placement; Fireman Dave, who drives the van; and Take-Away Dave, who brings his own Tupperware to reduce our reliance on single-use plastic.

Making tea and coffee behind the counter is a group of young people who joined us after one of our volunteers gave an assembly at their school. The group made a replica café using the online world-building game Roblox and when the real café is closed they meet virtually instead.

Ours is a local project seeking to provide solutions to a global problem. The carbon value of the food we intercept is 440 tons annually, the equivalent of a petrol car driven 2m miles. Across a year the volume of food we handle is equal in weight to 12 double-decker buses.

This is a minuscule fraction of the food that is wasted globally. Between 30 and 50% of food produced around the world goes into bins rather than bellies – more than enough to meet international food demand.

We talk a lot about value at REfUSE: the holy task of recognising the value of places, people and food that the governing political, cultural and economic systems have artificially drained of worth and designated as waste. We seek to acknowledge the carbon, time, labour and natural resources that are expended before food can reach our plates.

The efforts of each of our 200 volunteers are a challenge to the value judgements of large retail firms, such as Amazon, that devalue this food because its sell-by date

is built into their retail model. Hanging by the till in our community café is a sign that reads 'This food is not free! It's valuable. And so are you, so "pay as you feel", in money, time or skills.'

When people order meals, they are given an envelope in which they can contribute money or promises of time. It is posted anonymously into the payment box.

The whole exercise is entirely imperfect. We've had arguments in the kitchen, heroin needles in the bathroom and three different incidents of stolen money. Some give their widow's mite and others come in laden with glossy shopping-centre purchases and post back an empty envelope. I often find myself in conflict with the non-judgement that we claim is our guiding star. We are faced with the challenge of welcoming strangers who might have no interest in welcoming each other.

In the moments it works well, though, this recognition of value feels like the work of Jesus. His habit of exalting those who are humbled is mirrored when people peel wonky carrots and teach skills to young people with learning difficulties. His way of recognising people who have gone unrecognised by society is emulated by those who give so generously of themselves.

Allowing people to pay in the currency they have available changes the terms of the arrangement. It's an economy of grace. And like grace, it can be incredibly unfair. 'Pay as you feel' provides the same lunch to the

person who put £600 into our payment box last week and the person who consistently returns a handful of copper coins. Everyone becomes wealthy because the terms of wealth are made available to everyone.

All this happens against a backdrop of tension: we are working within an institution that we ultimately want to change, chasing glimpses of justice while hoping for a complete overhaul of an unjust system. Our business plan is to put ourselves out of business.

But for now, we come together, we chop, cook, serve and hope.

The Gift of Palliative Care

The Hawthorne Sisters serve terminal cancer patients, offering palliative care in the spirit of their founder.

Leah Libresco Sargeant

The Dominican order is a preaching order. White-habited friars and religious sisters teach theology, write books, operate schools – one friar even offered to chant the *Summa Theologica* during a pregnant friend's labour. (She declined.) But in Hawthorne, New York, the Dominican congregation of St Rose of Lima lives a quieter charism.

The sisters nurse terminal cancer patients. Their community was founded in 1900 by Rose Hawthorne Lathrop (the daughter of Nathaniel Hawthorne). Lathrop converted to Catholicism and took the religious name Mother Mary Alphonsa. She began by caring for incurable cancer patients on the Lower East Side of Manhattan and the congregation carries on that work today, outside the city.

Mim Skinner is a cofounder of REfUSE, which seeks to eliminate food waste and educate on its climate impact. She writes about female imprisonment, communal living and grief. Her books include Jailbirds: Lessons from a Women's Prison *(2019) and* Living Together *(2022).*

Their centre is certified for up to 54 patients, but they often serve about 25, since they stick to a more generous staffing ratio than the law requires. Their palliative care is marked by the gift of presence.

Some sisters are drawn to the congregation because they have already worked as nurses and they want a more prayerful life while continuing to serve the sick. For Sr Stella Mary, who entered the order 16 years ago, nursing had never been on her mind. She had imagined herself married, until God worked very strongly in her life and she knew she would enter religious life, but just didn't know *where*.

No matter their past expertise, all the sisters begin their formation in the religious life before they receive any medical training. A sister who enters with a medical degree might work as an assistant to an older sister who has more basic training as a certified nursing assistant. The new sister might be more practised at medicine, but not at the stillness and patience that the order cultivates. The sisters have the flexibility to set everything else aside to stay with a patient for as long as they are needed – very different from the rushed routines at many hospitals, that stretch nurses across too many patients.

Sr Stella Mary was nervous when she began working with patients, but older sisters gave her two pieces of advice. 'Remember, you are *first* a religious.' She would be trained in basic medical care, but her first work would always be to pray and love the patients. Nursing was a way to express that love. The other piece of advice was more practical – all the patients are terminal. She wouldn't be a surgeon whose smallest gesture could save a life or end it. Everyone came to the sisters to prepare to die and hopefully to die well.

When the patients arrive, Sr Stella Mary says, they come very broken, physically and emotionally. It's not just the knowledge that they are dying, but the fear of being a burden, the sorrow at not being able to take care of their families. Many come from hospitals that may have treated them as irritants. Because the patients are poor, they linger in hospitals long after a richer patient would be discharged. Their poverty means that most nursing facilities won't accept them, so they are stuck in limbo, unable to be safely discharged, until someone makes a call to the sisters.

For the sisters, there is no sense of regret about not knowing their patients as they were in their full strength. 'We don't have expectations "They always did this..."' Sr Stella Mary says. 'We're here to learn who they are at this point in time.' Their needs are how the sisters come to know them and the sisters' daily acts of service are the form their love takes. As Sr Stella Mary puts it, 'The people you remember the clearest are the ones who give you the most trouble.'

At each bedside, the sisters are preaching, just like their more famous and public brethren. While friars of the Thomistic Institute offer programmes on college campuses, the sisters are offering private tutorials on the nature of God.

To prepare for their work, they spend time in adoration of Jesus in the Eucharist. 'We receive God's love', Sr Stella Mary explains, and they let that love overflow from them. By looking at Jesus, they learn to see with his eyes. 'We love this person how God loves them, how God intends them to be loved.'

There are few direct citations of Saint Thomas Aquinas's *Summa*, but each act of care, each loving look, each unhurried moment of waiting together, is preaching. Here are your meds, here is who God is, here is who you are. Here I am with you, with him. ✒

Leah Libresco Sargeant's writing has appeared in the New York Times, First Things *and* FiveThirtyEight. *She runs* Other Feminisms, *a Substack community focused on interdependence.*

RANDALL GAUGER

In Search of Solace

A pastor who lost his son to cancer probes the problem of pain.

Note from the Editor: The suggestion for this 'Pain and Passion' issue came from my friend Randall Gauger a year ago. Since no good deed goes unpunished, I asked him to write the editorial introducing the issue. I can think of no better entry point to this topic than his essay below. —*Peter Mommsen*

AS I CONSIDER THE PROBLEM of pain, I am transported back to Australia in November 1999. My wife Linda and I were just beginning to feel at home in this six-month-old Bruderhof, Danthonia. As our little community looked towards the celebration of the first Advent together, we received the news that our 22-year-old son, Matt, living at a Bruderhof in Pennsylvania, had been diagnosed with an aggressive lymphoma. By the next day our church had arranged tickets back to the United States. We said little to each other during the 21-hour flight; we simply held hands and cried. We must have looked a sight getting off the plane with red and swollen eyes. We both felt numb. How could this be happening? Why, God?

By Christmas, Matt seemed to be responding to chemotherapy; in January, he married his fiancée,

Cynthia, who insisted that no amount of uncertainty or sickness would come in the way of their love. When cancer struck my son, I was stopped in my tracks. Everything changed in a moment, and the things I thought were important suddenly weren't. I was driven to prayer. I began to realise how shallow my life was, how little time I had actually spent focusing on the important things, and how little time each of us really has.

By March, Matt was doing so well that we returned to Australia. But just a few weeks later, the cancer was back, and we left Sydney once more, this time with the unspoken certainty that we were saying goodbye to our son. Same long flight, same tears.

It is unnatural to see your child die. There is something inside you that simply says, 'This should not be.' But being in that room when he left us,

Vincent van Gogh, *Pollard Willow*, gouache, ink and watercolour, 1882.

and hearing him speak of things he was seeing and feeling – things of heaven and eternity – changed us forever. Matt saw things that we could not see or fully comprehend, but for a few hours we glimpsed through him the other side of that door we will all go through one day.

Only a few years after Matt died, Linda was diagnosed with a rare and crippling autoimmune disease. It is characterised by fatigue, nerve pain and an array of other debilitating symptoms. The treatment is long-term steroids and immuno-suppressants, but naturally, they present their own challenges. Due to long-term steroid use, Linda has had six major back surgeries since 2015. Some-times, despite the doctors' best efforts, the pain simply cannot be controlled and she can't leave her bed. When Linda is fighting an especially tough bout and neither of us can really do anything about it, the frustration and discouragement threaten to overwhelm. There may be nothing tangible to be done, but we find ourselves turning more to other people for support, and to prayer.

As a pastor in the Bruderhof, I have been able to stand by other people who are in pain, whether emotionally or physically. Both Linda and I have the chance to do what others have done for us, and we now know firsthand that often the best thing you can do is to simply be a presence with those who are suffering. The worst thing is to come up with some practical answer or a suggestion that worked for someone else.

I often think of the story of Job. Everything is taken away from him: material possessions, family and health. Then his friends come along. They weep with him; they sit down in the dirt with him in silence for a whole week. But then they start talking and mess everything up! The apostle Paul has some simple and good advice for us: he says we ought to 'rejoice with those who rejoice, and weep with those who weep.'

Randall Gauger is a pastor in the Bruderhof communities. He and his wife, Linda, live at the Fox Hill community in New York.

Linda reminds me that sympathy cards and well-meant Bible quotes don't always strike at the right time. But if a true friend walks alongside, listens and occasionally shares words that uplifted him or her in a time of deep crisis, that can provide a bar to hold to when you feel as if you're drowning. Linda says:

After Matt's cancer diagnosis, a friend shared a passage from *Come Away My Beloved* by Frances

---

'If only my toothache would stop, I could write another chapter about pain.'
—*C S Lewis*

J Roberts with me – I still keep it inside my Bible. As I reflect on the loss of my son, something a mother will never 'get over', and the continual, grinding physical pain which can discourage me and beat me down, these words from that passage go through my mind almost daily: 'Bring your sorrow, and watch for the sunrise of resurrection... Hope is reborn and life finds new beginning. Wait for it as tulip bulbs anticipate the spring...God is mighty to save from despair, from sorrow, from disappointment, from regret, from remorse, from self-castigation, and from the hot, blinding tears of rebellion against fateful circumstances. He can save you from yourself, and He loves you when you find it hard to love yourself. Let His peace flow

Linda, Cynthia, Matt and Randall Gauger, December 1999.

in you like a river, carrying away all the poison of painful memories and bringing to you a fresh clear stream of pure life and restoring thoughts.

Yet Linda and I both know that sometimes there are no words, only tears. I look back on what I wrote for a book a friend compiled on Matt's life and death and I realise that in the intervening years, we have still found ourselves here:

I was keeping my concerns about Matt's situation bottled up because I was concerned that Linda was not handling things. The fact that I didn't really allow her to fully share her fears with me created a lot of tension. She needed me to identify with her and feel safe in confiding to me.

Then came that breakthrough, when I finally stopped keeping a wall up between us; when I allowed myself to become vulnerable. I realised that drawing into a shell in the face of Matt's illness could rip our marriage apart. We both knew of marriages where the pain and struggle that should draw husband and wife closer together actually did the opposite. Couples were driven apart by holding their feelings inside, distancing themselves from one another and speculating about what the other thinks and feels.

Suddenly, we were able to see our grief and stress mirrored in each other and we could share it openly with one another. We held each other and wept, for as long as we needed to. And then we could say, 'Well, that is enough for now, let's go on.' One day we could look at a picture of Matt and smile. The next day we'd see the same picture and totally fall apart. We didn't feel that we needed to deny or suppress what we felt, or that such emotions were wrong.

It was a tremendous relief to realise that we are not strong people; we are plain, ordinary people. And if we need to cry, then cry. If we need to grieve, then grieve. Do it hard and deeply, and then move on.

AS I REFLECT on my own experience of pain and consider the suffering of others, I have found an echo of my grief and questions in the writings of C S Lewis, who in his lonely sorrows put words to an experience shared by people across space and time – all of us, as he put it, 'ordinary privates in the huge army of the bereaved, slogging along and making the best of a bad job.'

At 10 years old, Lewis lost his mother to cancer. He had prayed to God for healing, and she died anyway. He became a convinced atheist. Then he experienced the trenches of World War I, including the death of his best friend and narrowly escaped death himself when an exploding bomb killed another soldier next to him. He endured increasing chronic pain as he got older. And he was devastated by the death of his wife, Joy, from cancer. By then a converted Christian, he grappled with God over her loss in the pages of his journal, pages that were eventually published as the 1961 book *A Grief Observed*.

Lewis's unanswered questions weighed him down: 'But go to Him when your need is desperate, when all other help is vain, and what do you find? A door slammed in your face and a sound of bolting and double bolting on the inside. After that, silence.' Many who have knelt in the depths of grief and agony will recognise this godforsakenness, this answerless void. Lewis articulates the same questions and fears that were roiling around in my own mind:

Aren't all these notes the senseless writings of a man who won't accept the fact that there is nothing we can do except to suffer it?...It doesn't really matter whether you grip the arms of the dentist's chair or let your hands lie in your lap. The drill drills on...Not that I am (I think) in much danger of ceasing to believe in God. The real danger is of coming to believe such dreadful things about him. The conclusion I dread is not 'So, there is no God

after all', but 'So this is what God is really like. Deceive yourself no longer.'

The greatest terror, then, wouldn't be to find that there is no God, but rather to find that he's there – and is, in Lewis's words, 'the Cosmic Sadist'. What good could so much senseless suffering possibly accomplish? And if such cries could be uttered by the man whose writings had so shaped my own spiritual growth and faith in God's goodness, what was left for me to hold on to? As someone who has suffered and watched my loved ones suffer, as a pastor who has mourned with those who are mourning, the answers to these questions – or at least answers that move beyond religious platitudes to provide solace and closure to the fearful and grieving – seem alarmingly elusive.

THE FIRST GLIMMER of an answer comes to Lewis here:

But suppose that what you are up against is a surgeon whose intentions are wholly good. The kinder and more conscientious he is, the more inexorably he will go on cutting. If he yielded to your entreaties, if he stopped before the operation was complete, all the pain up to that point would have been useless.

He is no longer hammering on a door that was slammed shut:

When I lay these questions before God I get no answer. But rather a special sort of 'No answer'. It is not the locked door. It is more like a silent, certainly not uncompassionate, gaze. As though he shook his head, not in refusal but waiving the question. Like, 'Peace, child; you don't understand.'

Ultimately, Lewis believed that heaven is the answer to the problem of pain. He held on to passages like 2 Corinthians 4: 'Therefore we do not lose heart. Though outwardly we are wasting away, yet inwardly we are being renewed day by day. For our light and momentary troubles are achieving for us an eternal glory that far outweighs them all. So we fix our eyes not on what is seen, but on what is unseen, since what is seen is temporary, but what is unseen is eternal.'

These are words that each of us have to encounter in our own time. They can't be lectured to us by a well-meaning counsellor, or embossed onto a sympathy card that arrives while we're struggling to take another breath, to make it through another hour. Yet they were written by someone who was himself wasting away, and communicated hope to others through his pain. I believe with Lewis and the apostle Paul that, as we fix our eyes on someone unseen, his gaze is fixed upon us, steady, unwavering, loving. We may only feel his hands when he reaches out, as he did to Matt, to bring us into his eternal light. Until then, we trust in his look to hold us. ⤜

Vincent van Gogh, *Orchard in Bloom with Poplars*, oil on canvas, 1889.

BENJAMIN
CROSBY

Ten Thousand 'Gentle' Killings

Where is the church in Canada's euthanasia experiment?

'If in a hundred years, Christians are identified as the people who don't kill their children or kill their elders we will have done well.' —Stanley Hauerwas

'**C**HURCH SHOULD NOT oppose MAID law, primate says.' So reads a recent headline of the *Anglican Journal*, the newspaper of the Anglican Church of Canada. In the piece, Archbishop Linda Nicholls calls for the church she leads to avoid publicly opposing the expansion of euthanasia, or medical assistance in dying (MAID), in Canada. 'The mood in Canada' is not 'to consider what churches have to say about this', she says, warning against 'imposing Christian values'. Far better for the church to 'focus on providing pastoral care to people who are considering medical assistance in dying', the article paraphrases her as saying, 'ensuring they have the support they need to make decisions based on the value of their life'.

The value of their lives is just what many fear would *not* be protected by the widespread adoption of euthanasia, so rapid and sweeping that the United Nations Special Rapporteur on the Rights of Persons with Disabilities has raised concerns.

Meanwhile, Archbishop Nicholls, the leader of one of Canada's largest and historically most influential Christian denominations, is arguing that on an issue of profound moral gravity, the church lacks the capacity and will to say anything to the public as a whole, or indeed even to offer definitive guidance to its own members. The most the church will do is solicit essays for a new collection of theological reflections on MAID and put out an editorial by Archbishop Nicholls expressing 'concern' about potential further MAID expansion while emphasising the church's role as a nonjudgemental provider of pastoral care. In this refusal to speak plainly, the church in which I serve is sadly not alone.

How did we get here? Euthanasia, which as of 2021 had become the sixth leading cause of death in Canada, was only legalised in 2016, in response to a 2015 Supreme Court of Canada ruling that criminalising euthanasia violated the Canadian Charter of Rights and Freedoms. The Canadian Parliament complied by passing Bill C-14, a law that allowed euthanasia in a set of carefully delineated circumstances: the person requesting it must have a 'grievous and irremediable medical condition' that is incurable, irreversible and involves unendurable suffering, in which 'natural death has become reasonably foreseeable.' Furthermore, consent at the time of the person's death was required, as was a 10-day waiting period. Children and those whose only diagnosis was mental illness were not eligible.

Disability rights groups and other concerned citizens spoke up in opposition to this law before and after its passage, but for advocates of MAID, within just a few years the existing law was seen as unduly constraining. Once again, the courts led the way: in 2019, the Superior Court of Quebec found that the 'reasonably foreseeable' stipulation in the government's euthanasia law violated the Charter. Parliament passed a new, more expansive MAID law in 2021. Not only did this law, called C-7, remove some of the stipulations for the killing of those whose natural deaths were reasonably foreseeable ('Track 1' euthanasia), but it also allowed people unlikely to die naturally in the near future to seek euthanasia too ('Track 2'). This means that euthanasia, which was initially argued for primarily in terms of terminally ill people for whom MAID would painlessly hasten an inevitable, rapidly approaching death, was now available for those nowhere near dying. The number of euthanasia deaths has grown dramatically each year, from 1,018 in 2016 to 10,064 in 2021. Over 3% of deaths in Canada as a whole in 2021 were via MAID.

Euthanasia is logistically distinct from 'assisted suicide', increasingly available in many Western countries including parts of the United States, which requires the individual's participation in swallowing lethal drugs. With euthanasia, a doctor injects them directly – a procedure that can be performed on individuals who are immobile or even unconscious. While MAID encompasses both methods of hastening death, over 99% of Canadian deaths under the law are via euthanasia.

Law C-7 also repealed the exclusion of stand-alone mental illness from the acceptable criteria for seeking MAID, to come into effect in early 2023. That is, supposedly incurable depression and other mental disorders will soon be grounds for a person to be killed by a doctor. (At the time of writing in February, the government has introduced legislation to delay by one year, but not repeal, this part of the expansion.) The government is currently exploring further loosening MAID access, including for so-called 'mature minors', and allowing euthanasia via advance directives, which would allow for individuals to ensure that they were killed via MAID if they were to suffer certain conditions – even if they withheld consent at the time that death would be administered.

MEANWHILE, an entire infrastructure has sprung up around MAID, that euphemises the procedure as gentle and nonthreatening. Thus you can find 'death doulas' who work with MAID patients and their families and friends, counselling those about to die to dress warmly and hydrate before their deaths and encouraging the bereaved to process the experience through grounding themselves in their bodies or expressing themselves through dance. What is actually going on – a doctor killing a patient – is cloaked in anaesthetising therapeutic language, presumably to make the experience more pleasant for everyone involved.

In sharp contrast to this gentle language that seeks to make death seem not so very terrible, proponents of MAID expansion use rather grimmer language to talk about the lives of the disabled and dying. They talk about experiences of dependence, nappies or drooling as evidence of a life lacking in dignity – and thus a life that should be allowed to be ended by doctor-delivered death. It is not a stretch to see why disabled advocates have argued that the expansion of MAID sends the message that 'simply having a disability is reason enough for us to want to die', that life with a disability is necessarily a life unworthy of being lived. Their fears are already coming to pass.

In 2021, the first year the 'reasonably foreseeable natural death' criterion was lifted, more than 200 Canadians who did not have a terminal illness ended their lives with MAID. This group was younger and more likely to use disability services than those with foreseeable deaths. Many reports have emerged of people pursuing MAID because they cannot access the support services they need to live a decent life or because they are pressured to do so by their medical providers. Here are just a few of them.

'Sophia', a 51-year-old woman who suffered

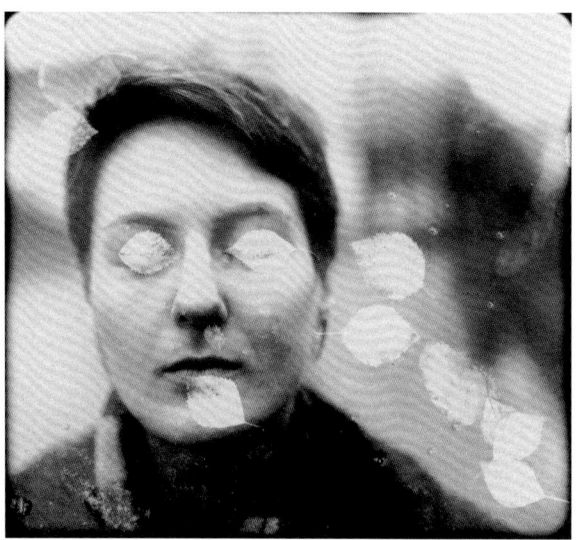

from multiple chemical sensitivities (MCS), could not obtain a flat that would meet her needs. While MCS is difficult to manage, symptoms can improve significantly with decent housing. 'The government sees me as expendable trash, a complainer, useless and a pain in the ass', she said in a video a few days before she was killed via MAID in February 2022.

'Denise', a 31-year-old, was pursuing MAID for similar reasons until a GoFundMe campaign bought her some time. But if she cannot find affordable housing going forward, she may still end up dying by euthanasia.

'Kat', a woman in her late 30s with a genetic disorder, cannot afford her treatments. 'I feel like I'm falling through the cracks so if I'm not able to access health care am I then able to access death care?' she told CTV News. She has been approved for what she calls an 'open invitation' to go through with MAID at any time.

Alan, a 61-year-old man, was hospitalised for suicidality and, within a month, applied for MAID. He was killed over the objections of family members and his primary medical provider, who

---

Benjamin Crosby is a priest in the Episcopal Church serving in the Anglican Church of Canada and a doctoral student in ecclesiastical history at McGill University, Quebec. The views expressed here are his own.

alleged that he did not understand MAID and was coerced into it by hospital staff. The only condition listed on his MAID application was hearing loss.

Sathya, a 44-year-old woman who suffered from motor neurone disease but for whom natural death was not imminent, was killed via MAID because she could not access home care. 'Ultimately, it was not a genetic disease that took me out, it was a system', she wrote shortly before her death in October 2022.

Some medical professionals even bring up euthanasia unprompted as an option for patients, including as a component of conversations about the costs of hospital stays, and there are regular reports of disabled people, given the insufficient state of disability benefits in Canada, considering MAID because of poverty. The implicit proffer of MAID as a solution to poverty and disability is a grievous betrayal of many of the values Canadians hold dear, of the laudable Canadian commitment to a kinder and gentler society that I have come to so admire as an immigrant here.

Even as these tragic and alarming stories come to light, the trajectory towards more permissive MAID rules seems unlikely to be reversed any time soon. Not only MAID for 'mature minors'

and via advance directives are on the horizon: a representative of the influential Quebec College of Physicians recently called for parents to be allowed to euthanise infants younger than one year in certain cases, declaring that MAID 'is not a moral, political or religious issue. It is a medical one.' And when the doctors have decided, who are we to judge?

One infamous clash between such 'medical' and moral values came to a head in 2019 when Dr Ellen Wiebe, a prominent MAID provider who has called her more than 400 euthanasia procedures the most rewarding part of her work as a doctor, sneaked into a Jewish care home to clandestinely kill a resident over the objections of home staff who warned that it might traumatise Holocaust survivors. The home filed a complaint with the province's College of Physicians and Surgeons, that cleared Wiebe of any wrongdoing – 'a decision I was expecting because I trust the College', she commented. Wiebe has also gained notoriety for telling other MAID providers that she arranged the reassessment of a person judged incompetent to seek MAID and then killed him. Are these actions really the sort of thing over which only the doctors performing them should have the final say?

To THEIR GREAT SHAME, Canadian mainline Protestants, the historic bastions of public Christianity in Anglophone Canada, have utterly failed to speak prophetically to the broader Canadian society or even coherently to their own members since the passing of MAID legislation in 2016. While many of these church bodies opposed euthanasia before its legalisation, since then they have consistently avoided taking strong positions on it, essentially conceding the Quebec doctors' argument that MAID is at base a medical issue, not a religious one. They have largely embraced a role of providing value-neutral 'pastoral care' in whatever end-of-life choices their people may make. But this sort of neutrality proves impossible to maintain. By abandoning their teaching authority, the churches end up supporting MAID advocates' accounts of human dignity and worth as bound up in choice and independence – accounts that are contrary to Christian teaching and death-dealing to disabled people.

These churches were not always so unwilling to take a stand. In 1996, the Faith and Witness Commission of the Canadian Council of Churches produced a statement critical of moves towards legalising euthanasia, while admitting that this 'convergence' was shared by 'many member Churches' but not necessarily all. The Anglican Church of Canada produced a 1998 report called *Care in Dying*, arguing that 'we believe that respect for persons would not be well served by a change in law and practice to enable a physician, family member or any private citizen to take the life of another or assist in their suicide.' However, despite what appears to be a straightforward judgement, *Care in Dying* uses some carefully hedged language that anticipates the moves the Anglicans and other mainline denominations would make in years to come: the report describes itself as 'a pastoral guideline rather than a policy statement', inviting 'thoughtful and prayerful engagement with the realities that people may face at the end of their lives rather than demanding obedience to closely defined teaching.' It is, unfortunately, precisely this nervousness about the church's power to teach and expect (or even ask for) obedience that would come to define most later mainline engagement with euthanasia.

Since 2016, the United Church of Canada, the Anglican Church of Canada and the Evangelical Lutheran Church in Canada (ELCIC) have all accepted MAID with varying degrees of enthusiasm. The United Church, Canada's largest Protestant denomination, produced a 2017 statement that 'we are not opposed in principle to the legislation allowing assistance in dying' and that MAID 'may be chosen as a faithful option in certain circumstances.' The ELCIC goes even further, declaring in its 2019 statement, 'We affirm that everyone has the human right to assistance in dying', assistance that explicitly includes euthanasia. Moreover, while the United Church released a follow-up statement in 2020 rejecting the expansion of MAID to those suffering solely from mental illness, as well as the practice of advance directives, the Lutherans instead expressed thanks that 'fortunately' the federal government had promised to expand MAID in precisely these ways! After all, the Lutherans affirm that providing access to MAID is a means of 'loving your neighbour', somewhat bizarrely quoting as supporting evidence Luther's explication of the fifth commandment that Christians must 'neither endanger nor harm the lives of our neighbour, but instead help and support them in all of life's needs'. Euthanasia, the ELCIC declares, is simply part of 'a respectful treatment plan developed under difficult circumstances with the best interests and the desires of our neighbour in mind'.

The Anglicans chose silence. To be sure, they had their own report, a 2018 follow-up to *Care and Dying* called *In Sure and Certain Hope* – an odd name for a statement so lacking in certainty of any kind. Unlike the United Church and the Lutherans, the Anglicans are unwilling to affirm explicitly that MAID can in some circumstances be a faithful choice. This is not because of any grave moral qualms, but seemingly because even such an affirmation would be too explicit a moral judgement. The church, the report declares, has 'become increasingly sceptical of our capacity to understand and interpret the work of God in the life of another person'. *Any definitive judgement about the meaning of a person's life* is off limits to the church – rather, the church simply must 'listen in the encounter between God and the patient'. The church's job is to help the dying 'continue to experience meaning, purpose and control over one's life', facilitating whatever decisions they wish to make and 'be[ing] present'. While the report encourages caregivers to seek to 'build bridges between the stories told by the parishioner and the stories/teachings of Christ', certainly any authoritative pronouncement about the nature of life or death seems out of bounds.

In practice, such studied neutrality ends up endorsing the broader Canadian culture's approach to and understanding of euthanasia, even at the points where such understanding is incompatible with Christian faith. For example, the United Church includes several prayers for use by those planning to end their lives via MAID on the 'Death and Dying' section of the church website, co-written by a United Church minister and an executive of Dying with Dignity, the largest pro-euthanasia advocacy group. One of the prayers, designed for a person experiencing fear, includes the following:

I hope they [my family] will be proud of my decision and will understand that MAID is consistent with the love and compassion of Jesus. I have such peace in knowing this is my choice.

Consider too a second prayer, for deciding on the time and place of death:

I do not want to linger in pain, waiting for death to come. I do not want my family and loved ones to watch me suffer to the bitter end. I do not want them to be haunted by memories of a slow, painful death. Daily my dignity is being eroded. I am ready to go through that final door. *I give thanks that I have still the ability to choose, but I realise this window of lucid opportunity may very soon be closed* [emphasis original].

What these prayers show us is that a supposedly neutral, nonjudgemental approach to accompanying the dying in whatever choice they happen to make actually involves supporting and reinforcing a whole range of judgements about what a good life and a good death consist in. The valorisation of choice as the central component of a meaningful life and the suggestion that the suffering of serious illness includes an erosion of dignity are characteristic of pro-MAID language in Canada. It is worth adding explicitly that the association of illness or disability with the loss of human dignity found in the second prayer is precisely what disability advocates have been warning broader Canadian society about: surely one does not lose one's dignity by being disabled or seriously ill! Churches that choose – in contradiction to the entire history of Christian pastoral care – to forgo any sort of strong moral judgement, failing to teach their people that some choices are right and others are wrong, end up simply parroting the messages of broader Canadian culture.

As the Presbyterian Church of Canada, the only mainline body that has maintained a consistent condemnation of euthanasia, stated in its 2017 statement on the topic, the catechesis about a valuable life from the broader Canadian culture is directly in opposition to Christian teaching. As the Presbyterians note,

We live in a culture enamoured with the closing lines of 'Invictus' by William Ernest Henley: 'I am the master of my fate: I am the captain of my soul.' 'Invictus' is a stirring work of literature, but it decries any trust in God. As Reformed Christians, we profess a different heritage, powerfully stirring to our souls, that proclaims a complete and utter trust in God.

In their refusal to combat the culture's discipleship of their members, the United Church and the Anglican and Lutheran churches have abandoned both public witness to those outside the church and the exercise of the teaching office to those within it. Instead, in the name of non judgemental pastoral presence, the churches are choosing to baptise the same values that have led to MAID's continued expansion and an ever-rising death count over the continued concerns of disability rights groups who rightly see the dignity and very lives of disabled persons under attack. Perhaps the most vivid image of the mainline churches' capitulation is a MAID death being carried out in the sanctuary of a United Church in Manitoba, complete with the minister telling journalists that there was a 'sense of "rightness"' in this woman's killing.

This, in the end, is where an ethic of sympathy and avoiding judgement absent clear moral commitments leads. For indeed we ought not doubt the deep sympathy with suffering and the humanitarian motives to ease it that drives the popular concern about end-of-life options. One might even say that it is an ethic of sympathy with specifically Christian roots in Jesus' particular concern for the poor, the suffering, the down-trodden. Yet it is an ethic of sympathy divorced from its original context within a Christian theological and anthropological framework, within a moral universe in independent self-fashioning is not the highest good. And without this framework, as we have seen in Canada, this ethic of sympathy can go terribly awry. As Flannery O'Connor puts it, 'when tenderness is detached from the source of tenderness [the person of Christ], its logical outcome is terror.'

THERE IS MUCH TO DESPAIR about concerning the current Canadian experiment with euthanasia and the mainline churches' surrender. But there are also reasons for hope. Roman Catholics, evangelicals, conservative confessional Protestants and other Christian groups have continued to publicly oppose MAID expansion, joining other religious communities and disability rights advocates standing against an ideology that sees independence as a necessary aspect of human dignity or a good human life. These groups witness in a Canadian context that dependence, far from being an unusual state to be shunned at all costs (even one's death!), is an inevitable and indeed *good* part of the human condition.

One of the most visible examples of Christians standing against MAID is in the 2020 open letter 'We Can and Must Do *Much* Better', in which evangelical, Pentecostal, confessional Protestant, Anabaptist, Roman Catholic and Orthodox leaders joined Jewish and Muslim leaders in decrying

MAID's expansion. The letter also offered an alternative vision of how Canadians might respond to the situations of profound suffering that may lead people to choose MAID, not least through expanding access to palliative care as an alternative to euthanasia. In short, the letter is a call to soli-darity: 'Rather than withdrawing from those who are not far from leaving us, we must embrace them even more tightly, helping them to find meaning up to the last moments of life.'

These churches have also worked to find common cause with nonreligious groups that have similarly opposed MAID expansion, especially the disability rights community. The Evangelical Fellowship of Canada's response focused on the particular harm MAID might do to the disability community and echoed the language of disability advocates in declaring that 'in Canada, it shouldn't be easier to have help in ending your life than to get the support and care you need to live'. Christian and disability rights organisations alike have been weighing in on Canada's current study about expanding MAID to mature minors and allowing it via advance directive.

But perhaps more important than tactical alliances is the way that these groups – otherwise quite different – find themselves articulating a similar account of what makes (or does not make) a full and dignified human life. As the Canadian Evangelical magazine *Faith Today* writes, paraphrasing the physician and professor Dr Margaret Cottle: 'It is not undignified to be cared for...If we believe every person is created in God's image, then they deserve such care.' That is, dependence, requiring the assistance of others to live one's life, does not do anything to detract from one's basic humanity – *pace* the United Church of Canada prayer that invites the suffering person to pray, 'Daily my dignity is being eroded.' Inclusion Canada, an organisation advocating for the rights of Canadians with intellectual disabilities, strikes the same tone in a more secular register, warning against the 'wide-scale perception that some persons' lives are not worth living.' Instead, the organisation seeks to promote 'positive narratives' about 'the quality of life of persons who live with disability, frailty and suffering'. Similarly, the Canadian Council on Disabilities has articulated its opposition to 'negative stereotypes about people with disabilities as suffering individuals in need of state-regulated assistance to end our lives.'

Whatever else they may agree or disagree on, here the traditional Christian account of what makes a good life corresponds very closely with those of disability rights advocates. The notion underlying much MAID advocacy – that a good, dignified life consists above all of independence, absence of suffering and the proliferation of choices – is contradicted by the experience of disabled persons asserting that their lives have value despite physical pain or the need for care from others, and despite any constraints upon their options. And for the Christian, it is contradicted too by our understanding of the good life as one of acknowledged dependence upon others and above all on God. The Presbyterians make this point powerfully by quoting the beginning of the Heidelberg Catechism in their MAID report:

> Q What is your only comfort in life and in death?
> A That I am not my own, but belong – body and soul, in life and in death – to my faithful Saviour, Jesus Christ.

For the Christian, if indeed Jesus Christ is our model of a fully human life and life in Christ is our goal, independence, freedom from suffering and the proliferation of choices simply cannot be the necessary requirements for a good life. And Christians can and must agree with secular disability rights advocates that any account of human dignity that places disabled people outside it because they need care is nothing less than evil.

'This is not the end of the road for us', stated Roxana Jahani Aval, chair of the Canadian Council on Disabilities, at the time of MAID expansion. 'This is a fight for our lives'. It is my hope that Christians will continue to accompany them in this struggle, not only Roman Catholics and evangelicals but even within the mainline churches as well. As an Anglican priest serving in the Anglican Church of Canada, I pray that my own church may repent of its silence, its collaboration with a death-dealing euthanasia system that is particularly hostile to the lives of disabled persons. May we stand for the dignity of all people and the goodness of our dependence upon each other – and upon God.

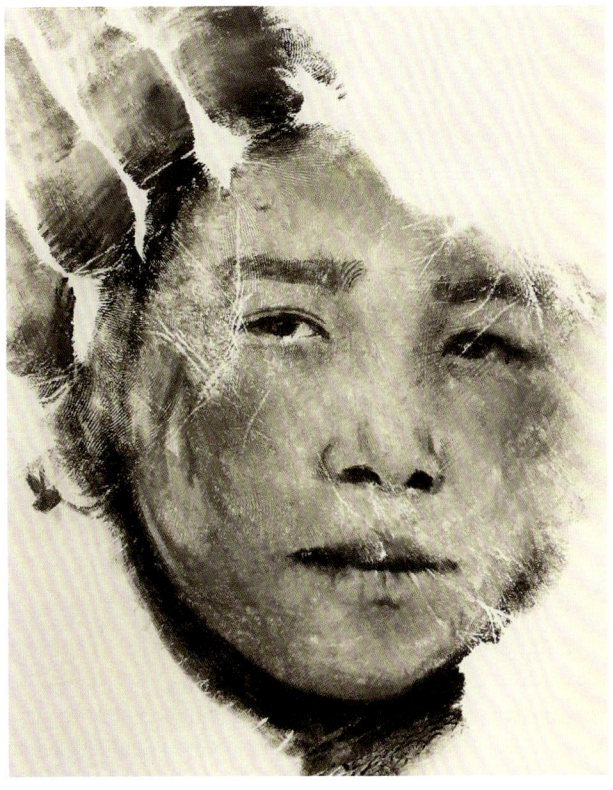

Saving Friends

*An insufferable patient teaches her doctor
a better approach to medicine.*

BREWER EBERLY

'I grasp the hands of those next me, and take my place in the ring to suffer and to work, taught by an instinct, that so shall the dumb abyss be vocal with speech.' —*Ralph Waldo Emerson*

I MET THE PATIENT I WILL CALL AMY early in my residency. 'She looks sick', our nurse told me, displaying a concerned look I had learned to trust. I walked into the examination room to meet a frail, middle-aged woman fervently pacing, tearful and wheezing through a dense miasma of perfume and cigarette smoke.

Amy presented with an unforgettable constellation of physical exam findings: bilateral ear infections, leukoplakia (white patches) on her tongue and a stab wound. She was homeless and the stab wound came from her boyfriend, who also provided the crystal meth she had smoked

unrecognisable: emaciated and brittle, and in terrible pain. We admitted her, in part, because she was threatening to take her own life. I visited her hospital room shortly after. She begged for our hospital's applesauce, which was the only food she could stomach. Her requests were peppered with a truly impressive repertoire of profanity, garbled by the surgical removal of part of her tongue. Even when she was asleep, the folds and furrows of her face seemed locked in an expression of bitterness and misery.

Amy was one of the few patients whom no one seemed to like. She was, literally, friendless. Even the most empathetic among us were seemingly unmoved by Amy. She was suffering, yes, but she had become insufferable.

MUCH HAS BEEN SAID ABOUT the 'epidemic of loneliness' in the West – the great unmooring of neighbourly life, the bewildering rates of anxiety, depression and 'deaths of despair' that seem dose-dependent on social media use, as some studies have suggested. This epidemic demands renewed attention to how, and whom, we befriend, especially in institutions such as hospitals that host human beings at their most vulnerable. The very idea of the hospital, after all, is born of the call towards *hospital*-ity and love of the poor and the stranger. But friendless patients like Amy press most clearly on the failure of contemporary medical ethics to inspire and sustain the moral imagination of medical trainees.

The classic framework of principlism taught in all medical schools, in its emphasis on the four principles of respect for autonomy, beneficence, non-maleficence and justice, leaves patients like Amy in a precarious place. On the wards, I remember, we repeated the word 'autonomy'

that morning. It was the oral leukoplakia that proved the most ominous; she was diagnosed soon after with metastatic cancer of the mouth and throat.

I've thought about Amy many times over the last few years. As a resident physician, I participated in her admissions and bounce-backs, working with fellow residents and faculty to coordinate social support and care. But a life of unhealth, addiction and violence led irrevocably to profound alienation from family, friends and medical resources. As if driven to the point of no return, Amy no-showed visits, left AMA (against medical advice) and refused to see specialists. We hung our heads as she was systematically kicked out of every boarding home and refuge in the area. Her family stopped answering our calls.

The last time I took care of Amy, she was almost

Brewer Eberly is a third-generation family physician at Fischer Clinic in Raleigh, North Carolina, and a McDonald Agape Fellow in the Theology, Medicine and Culture Initiative at Duke Divinity School.

Russell Powell, *Untitled*, mixed media with handprints.

frequently, as if to justify a Pyrrhic victory: she was dying, but at least we had maintained our principle. I remember someone saying, 'She made her bed; she can sleep in it.' I don't remember speaking up. I do remember vaguely nodding along.

Beneficence and non-maleficence were little help either. 'We've done everything we can possibly do' was repeated each morning, suggesting that the tasks of pursuing good and avoiding harm had been exhausted and the best we could hope for seemed to be the maintenance of the status quo. A senior resident on the team put it starkly: 'The best we can do in this situation is discharge her with pain control. She'll probably come back again in two weeks or die on someone's doorstep.'

As for justice, someone commented, in one of the team's most cynical and burnt-out moments, that the only '*just*' thing to do was to '*just* let her die'. Here was justice, cut down to an adverb. An older physician took it so far I still can't believe he said it aloud, a whiff of the hidden curriculum that still rots behind the closed doors of medicine: 'What we need here is not a TOC, "transition of care", but a TOB – "take out back."'

Such comments often come from clinicians who by all other accounts are competent and compassionate. They're often doctors who win teaching awards. I had heard the same physician call for renewed care for marginalised patients. And that is precisely the tension: there are some forms of suffering so abysmal, some patients so insufferable, that they reveal our ethical posturing. With Amy, we yielded to a dehumanising and grisly gallows humour because it made a kind of awful, dissonant sense. This was how we got through morning rounds when we realised we couldn't heal a patient.

How we conceive of autonomy, goodness and justice (or their absence) serves as a fulcrum to reimagine the care clinicians offer for patients like Amy. The philosopher Andreas Esheté argues that in the revolutionary triad of liberty, equality and fraternity, it is fraternity that serves as the scaffold for both liberty and equality. And yet, ironically, fraternity is the feature most likely to be omitted from modern descriptions of justice. In other words, in the context of a contemporary emphasis on personal fulfilment and social fairness, we eclipse the role of fraternity – mere friendship – in our pursuit of justice. With Amy and other insufferable patients, an emphasis on liberty and equality (autonomy and justice) proves inadequate. As Sheldon Vanauken writes in *Under the Mercy*, 'We can all agree that we ought to love our neighbours, except of course the awful ones we happen to have.'

But fraternity might breathe new life into our medical ethics. Aristotle says that a life without friends is not worth living, even a life possessed of 'all other goods', such as health, community or beauty (*Nicomachean Ethics*, 1155a). If so, then what about a life, like Amy's, stripped of all other goods and void of friendship?

The number of 'close friendships' in the United States has declined dramatically over the last three decades. According to the Survey Center on American Life, 12% of Americans reported they had no close friendships in 2021 compared with only 3% in 1990.

Of course, a medical ethic of fraternalism cannot mean what we popularly mean by friendship: emotional affection built on shared interests or experiences. Indeed, Aristotle famously categorised friendship into three types: friendships of utility, pleasure and virtue (*Nicomachean Ethics*, bk 7).

An ethic of fraternalism cannot be based on Amy's utility – what she might offer us, an interesting case history or clinical pearl perhaps. Amy's case may have been interesting at first, but we admitted her so many times that there seemed to be nothing left for us to learn from her. A fraternalism of pleasure was impossible; her care was far from enjoyable.

If an ethic of fraternalism is to contribute to the

moral imagination of medicine, it must be this third category, friendship of virtue – sometimes called a moral friendship – in which we commit to seek the good of the other regardless of the experience of caring for them, what they might offer us in return and perhaps especially what they 'deserve'.

It is easy to function as a medical meritocracy, in which the attention and care we offer to the suffering is contingent upon their effort, participation or 'compliance', and in which we commit to seek the good only insofar as the patient seeks the good too. The good doctor helps those who help themselves?

Whereas principle-based ethics may succeed when patients have the capacity and wherewithal to choose 'the good' for themselves, a medical ethic of fraternalism is more fitting when patients are confused, choosing poorly or not choosing at all. A medicine of moral friendship recognises that it is precisely those who consistently *do not* choose the good who may be most in need of accompaniment and healing.

A family member recently asked if it makes me angry 'when people don't take care of themselves'. I pointed out that patients who 'don't take care of themselves' are often burdened by other cares (such as taking care of others who can't take care of themselves). 'Self-care', a near-perfectly ironic term, is often available to the optimised elite who can afford yoga and counselling. Those who don't have a vision for bodily well-working – who are apathetic towards their creatureliness – are often the ones most in need of medicine. My family member wasn't convinced.

Later that night, we watched John Hughes's classic *Planes, Trains and Automobiles*, which struck me as an example of moral friendship with the insufferable and those who don't take care of themselves.

John Candy plays Del Griffith, an obese, overbearing shower-curtain-ring salesman with smelly feet and a long list of peccadilloes. Steve Martin plays Neal Page, a confident and chilly marketing executive just trying to get home for Thanksgiving. The movie's plot and humour hinge on Del and Neal continuing to cross paths, suffering together the misery of disrupted travel plans and forced companionship.

Planes, Trains and Automobiles is a subversive witness here, because it is the insufferable Del who steadfastly attempts to befriend. Del is clearly annoying, but Neal reveals his own sins in his self-assurance and entitlement. They're both insufferable, and it is in something like moral friendship (though they aren't 'buddies') that the film finds its enduring warmth and staying power.

It's interesting that Del is always talking about the friends he has made while selling shower curtain rings, while Neal never mentions a single friend. Del is eager to share the unexpected assets of his connections. Neal just wants to pay and be done with it.

But something about Del's presence begins to slowly soften Neal. It is over a cramped meal that Neal says offhand, 'I'm spending too much time away from home', foreshadowing Neal's thanks to Del near the end of the film: 'You got me home…a little late…but I'm a little wiser too.' What happens next – when Neal finally gets on his long-awaited subway ride home, puts all the pieces together and returns to find Del sitting alone in a train station – is one of the most poignant scenes in comedy film. Roger Ebert gave it four stars, calling it a 'moral rebirth' akin to Scrooge's in *A Christmas Carol*:

> The movies that last, the ones we return to, don't always have lofty themes or Byzantine complexities. Sometimes they last because they are arrows straight to the heart. When Neal unleashes that tirade in the motel room and Del's face saddens, he says, 'Oh. I see.' It is a moment that not only defines Del's life, but is a turning point in Neal's, because he also is a lonely soul and too well organised to know it.

I HAVEN'T FORGOTTEN ABOUT AMY. She was an arrow straight to the heart of what we were doing in medicine. She continues to reveal to me how strangely lonely we are in medicine and 'too well organised to know it'.

What did a medicine of moral friendship mean for Amy? It didn't mean that we sat in her room swapping stories with her. Most of her tongue had been removed; we spoke very little. We understood there are distinctions between fraternisation and an ethic of fraternalism.

What fraternity did mean was that the team did not sacrifice Amy on the altar of her own autonomy. We stopped speaking in terms of her merit – as a vagabond who deserved her state and did not deserve our medicine. But this took explicitly naming all I've said above, interrogating it candidly in community, repenting over what we had said, disrupting the momentum of morning rounds to point towards a different way of treating and speaking about the insufferable. Amy forced us to ask crucial questions we should have been asking long before: What are we doing here again? Who are we becoming? What is medicine for...and *who* is medicine for?

Medicine can be lonely. And I hate to say that we often transmit that loneliness. I think we tried to look at Amy, in all her fragility and mutuality, as a moral friend – unrecognisable in her suffering, perhaps, but no less worth our attention and fumbling attempts at forbearance. At the very least, this ethic of fraternalism allowed us to take a moral breath, fostering a kind of candour to name the paradoxes of her care and the care of many others we struggle to heal: we can't keep caring for you; we will keep caring for you. Yes, you are responsible for some of this; some of this you are not responsible for. No, you're not going to get better; no, we won't abandon you.

I don't know what happened to Amy or where she is now. I have no peaceful ending to offer here. We eventually discharged her and she was admitted

shortly after to a different hospital. I stopped following her care, but she has followed me.

The poet and paediatrician William Carlos Williams writes, 'There's nothing like a difficult patient to show us ourselves.' Amy, in all her suffering and insufferableness, shows us to ourselves. And sometimes what we see is not pleasant. Our reflection is just as broken and in need of friendship as the friendless patient who revealed it to us in the first place. What we do at the limits of our medical ethics reveals what kind of medicine it is that we are being formed to practise.

My wife was once driving with our sons. As they passed the hospital, she said, 'That's where your daddy works!' My youngest son, all of two years old, declared, 'He's a doctor!' My wife asked him what doctors do, to which he replied, 'They have friends.' Laughing, she asked him again, 'Yes, but what do they *do*?' My son answered, 'They save friends.'

What a beautiful imagination. ≥

Russell Powell, *Hold On*, mixed media with handprints.

Sep 3, 2010

...friend, Lisi,

...eep for knowing that you haven't
...tten to you since mid-August!

...Wednesday night we had such a
...long evening with your mom and dad
...dad had concocted a fantastic meal, a
...tomatoes mixed with all kinds of herbs
...ngs I can't remember now, plus a side dish
...fresh from the ground -- this might not sound
...was. And the whole evening
...re from Wesley Jackson (I
...y when your dad reads) an
...der, Rubbi-Kub, three-thi
...mom won hands down as she
...take it for granted and don'
...once said, "I am still a man,'
...when he said it.
    I think of you sitting at
...dealing with shipping problems a
...goes with that, and overseeing CP
...you see how I carry your work load on
...load to my load is a heavy load, let me t
...to admit that my load is light in comparison.

LETTERS FROM A VANISHING FRIEND

What's it like to succumb to Alzheimer's?
The story of an epistolary friendship.

LISABETH BUTTON

I LAID MY FIVE-DAY-OLD BABY DOWN
next to Ellen on her hospital bed. Ellen, age 85,
had been unresponsive for the past few days,
barely eating or drinking. Her room, filled with
family, caretakers, flowers and an overpowering
scented candle, seemed almost uncannily
peaceful – so different from the happy energy of
Ellen's home on my many previous visits. As I sat
next to her bed and held her hand, I reflected on
the improbable friendship that had blossomed
between my then-teenage self and the remarkable
mind now trapped by Alzheimer's – her helplessness so similar to the helplessness of my newborn
daughter.

I WAS 16 YEARS OLD WHEN OUR
paths were placed in each other's way. Certainly,
I was not looking for a friend in her 70s, and she
didn't really need me – her six living children and
their families all adored her, and her dozens of
grandchildren were constantly visiting. But when
she and her husband Ulrich, 'Ullu', who were old
friends of my parents, moved into the flat next to
our family, they became part of our daily lives. (In
a Bruderhof house, each family has their own flat,
but hallway and kitchen space may be shared.) My
parents expected my seven older siblings and me
to show Ullu and Ellen the same love and respect
we gave our grandparents, even if this translated

into long Scrabble games on the nights when I had
the most homework.

This wasn't actually much of a hardship: Ellen
was terrific company. She loved to laugh, and to
laugh with Ellen meant being reduced to helpless
wheezing. She was an attentive hostess and
conversationalist, brimming with interest in her
fellow humans. Evenings in our houses were for
conversation, board games, reading aloud (James
Thurber, Damon Runyon, the poems of Jane
Kenyon), with snacks and drinks prepared and
served with great courtesy by Ullu, and a revolving
cast of friends joining in. It was a wonderful time,
and Ellen didn't like to see it being interrupted
even for a couple of days, welcoming our family
home from a weekend trip with a typed note:

Dear Marcus & Monika and every single
one of you dear people,

We hope—and know—that you had a
wonderful time together, but you might
think again before you do this to us.

My God (excuse me) please think twice
and consider our feelings. We are pretty
fragile people. You can't play around with
our feelings. Will you remember that and
will you take it to heart? What if you
came home and found us lying spread out
on your floor, panting? Wouldn't you feel
a little bit sorry? A little remorse?

So don't do this again lightly, at least not
all of you at the same time. Leave one of
you at home. What about Lisabeth? You
wouldn't miss her that much, would you?
She's not around very much anyways
and I need her more than you do.

Take this to heart. One day, like on a Sunday, might be all right, maybe. But no more than one day. And you know, I had such a longing for a game of Rummikub, even though Marcus cheats. My hand is shaking, that's why I have to type.

Your Ellen

Considering that at the time, I was consumed by all things adolescent (music, novels, boys), it seems odd that Ellen befriended me so quickly and I am not entirely sure why or when it happened. It may have started when my mum asked me to help Ellen clean her house every Saturday morning. Ellen would watch me work from her rocking chair and the invariable discussion about what books I was reading made one hour quickly ooze into two. I learned never to walk into her house without an answer prepared for, 'So what are you reading now?' and learned also to be prepared to be chastised if I accidentally mentioned the John Grisham novel I had just picked up or some thrilling romance. '*That's* not a book!' she would say with withering disdain and I would once again be urged to try one of her favourites: *War and Peace*, *The Brothers Karamazov* or *Pride and Prejudice* ('Someday, you too shall find your own Mr Darcy', she would say with a twinkle).

Or it may have begun when I started helping her count out her pills for the week – she had recently been diagnosed with Alzheimer's on top of her existing health issues and found sorting the myriad little pills into the pill-counter difficult. Or perhaps it was our weekly outing to the local sauna (according to her, some form of therapy),

during which, despite her horrific heart condition, she would plunge into the pond's icy water on the coldest of winter days. However it happened, Ellen somehow had a way of understanding and listening to a 16-year-old who was otherwise quite preoccupied with teenage drama.

I didn't notice that as the months wore on, Ellen's Alzheimer's was progressing, inflicting psychological pain as a result. For all her cheer, Ellen was no stranger to suffering. Earlier in life she had lost her two youngest children: three-year-old Mark John from a brain tumour, then only seven months later two-month-old Marie Johanna due to the aftermath of a traumatic birth during which Ellen's heart had stopped for several minutes. 'I think such an experience can make you or break you, and it nearly broke me', she wrote decades later. 'My grief and pain accompanied me through the nights and the

---

Lisabeth Button lives at the Woodcrest Bruderhof, New York, with her husband and three children. She teaches literature and history to seventh and eighth grade students.

days for – well, for too long considering that I was a Christian and knew where Mark John was and that our aching loss was his unfathomable gain. Only years later I was able to let go of him and then I was able to experience that the sorrow had actually turned into a blessing for our whole family.'

Although Ellen had often told me about these two children, my inexperienced heart couldn't comprehend how much pain their loss caused her. But this familiarity with pain helped her now as memory loss forced her to relinquish the much-loved editing work she had done for decades. Other losses followed, including our weekly visits to the sauna when she became unable to walk that far or would forget why we were going in the first place. Yet none of this diminished our friendship.

WHEN I LEFT HOME AFTER SECONDARY school, our conversations were transformed into an exchange of letters. I kept hers, hundreds of pages typed on a manual typewriter.

> Dear Lisabeth, I miss you terribly. I mourn for myself and for the dishrag I have become. Limp and damp. And it's because the house is unbearably empty without you and your mom and dad. We were still smarting from your hegira (means 'your disappearance'–I looked it up in the dictionary) and then this–your mom and dad's hegira! My stomach was churning and my heart was beating irregularly on the eve of their departure and it has not lifted. As I write, my heart is palpitating. Maybe I'll have a heart attack and then everybody will be sorry! (I hope).

Every once in a while, my parents would let me know how Ellen was really doing – the panicked moments of forgetfulness that became more regular; the days that she would spend in her bedroom, held down by a dark depression. But like many sufferers of Alzheimer's, she often masked her pain well and this daily fight with her disease mostly didn't appear in the stream of letters, that arrived once, twice or sometimes even three times a week.

> I just finished *War and Peace* for the second or third time. It's a fantastic work. I guess you've read it. (Or are you still reading *Sue Barton, Student Nurse*?? Sorry).

> * * *

> Today is Friday and on Wednesday night we had such a great family supper and long evening with your mom and dad. Your dad had concocted a fantastic meal, a concoction of cooked tomatoes mixed with all kinds of herbs and spices and things I can't remember now, plus a side dish of new potatoes fresh from the ground–this might not sound special but it was. And the whole evening was special. Your dad read more from Wesley Jackson (I LOVE Wesley Jackson, especially when your dad reads) and afterwards we played, in this order, Rummi-Kub, Three-Thirteen, and then 10,000, which your mom won hands-down as she always does. But your dad and I take it for granted and don't feel inferior–as your dad once said, 'I am still a man', which nearly broke my heart when he said it.

> * * *

> Lisabeth, it's unconscionable. (I just looked up that long word in the diction-ary. I had spelled it wrong but now it's right. I'm not sure what it means. By the

way, while I was looking up the spelling
in the U pages, I happened across a
word that seemed to me to be of some
importance – 'unhouselled' – which means
'not having received the Eucharist, esp.
shortly before death.' Now that's pretty
serious. We have to take it to heart.

Well, that's all I can think of for now.
Auf Wiedersehen (not goodbye) my
dearest and best friend. I love you.

Ellen

AS TIME PASSED AND I ENTERED MY EARLY
20s, she remained the optimist; her letters always
encouraged me to keep going, work harder,
believe more – though they now took on a new
tone. In a way, just as Ellen's mind was taking
her to an unfamiliar place, so was our friendship
unexpectedly taking me to a new, deeper place
of faith. Ellen's own youthful reading had started
her on a path that led her from agnostic Judaism
to Christianity and eventually to the Bruderhof.
As other pillars of her life wobbled and then fell
to the encroaching disease, she clung ever more
tightly to these earlier foundations. She repeatedly
referenced Father Zosima's exposition on the
'Great Idea' in *The Brothers Karamazov* – that 'true
security is to be found in social solidarity rather
than in isolated individual effort' and that 'all
will suddenly understand how unnaturally they
are separated from one another.' For this, 'a man
must set an example, and so draw men's souls
out of their solitude and spur them to some act of
brotherly love'. Such passages had convinced Ellen

that living a life of brotherhood was the answer to
society's problems and I knew she hoped that I too
would find this same cause worth living for.

While I struggled along a new path towards
discipleship, Ellen continued to encourage me
from a place of unconquered faith:

Ullu and I have been thinking a lot
about the words of Jesus to seek first
the kingdom of God and then all the
other things will be added. And I'm
experiencing the truth and reality of
that promise. When I really focus on
Jesus, everything falls into the right
perspective.

The thought is so great that the future
kingdom can be with us, that we can be
united already with God's kingdom which
is eternal, that Jesus can and wants to
lead us as king here and now and in the
future.

There's so much more to write, but I'd
better stop now.

And a few days later:

A P.S. to my last letter. You asked what
my vision is of the kingdom of God. You
know I experienced heaven while Marie
Johanna was being born. I know it wasn't
the kingdom of God, but it was beautiful.
It says in Revelations that when the
kingdom of God breaks in on earth, 'the
dwelling of God will be with men, he

will dwell with them, and they shall be his people, and God himself will be with them...He will wipe away every tear from their eyes, and death will be no more, neither shall there be mourning nor crying nor pain any more'.

I can't tell you how much that meant to me when Mark John died. I turned to those words again and again, also the well-known words in Corinthians: 'Lo, I tell you a mystery, we shall not all sleep, but we shall all be changed...for the trumpet will sound and the dead will be raised imperishable'," and then the most wonderful words, 'Death is swallowed up in victory. O death, where is thy sting?'

Once again, the timing of her letters was perfect: my personal faith was at full ebb as I struggled to come to terms with the neurological symptoms of Lyme meningitis, at that time a very misunderstood disease. Only Ellen seemed to comprehend what I was going through in a way that none of my peers or my parents could. At one point, her weekly letter related the message of that week's worship meeting as an encouragement:

At our morning meeting we prayed for protection and healing according to God's will. Michael [the minister] read the story of how Peter walked on the water towards Jesus, and when he was afraid of sinking and cried out to Jesus for help, Jesus reached out his hand. Lisabeth, you are walking on the water now, and you know that we love you dearly and pray for you for protection and healing. One of your best friends, Ellen.

MEANWHILE, ELLEN HERSELF WAS deteriorating. Because of her heart condition, she experienced several brushes with death. 'I got halfway up there once, don't bring me back now', she said to a doctor during one of these episodes, referring to Marie Johanna's birth. Later, as she lay in bed with her family around her, singing their favourite hymns, my sister came in to say what she thought was goodbye. Ellen clasped her hand and whispered, 'I can't sit up now, but you'll find a new Dorothy Sayers on the bottom shelf there.' (She recovered, and later said that she had decided she was glad to still be on earth.)

On the good days, she still came to the community's woodworking factory for several hours to socialise with other people her age while doing simple handwork. She attended communal meals and participated in worship meetings. She visited newborn babies and held them close, singing snatches of lullabies in tiny ears. In winter, she asked to be taken sledging long after she couldn't walk. And for as long as she could, she remained the hostess, inviting other older ladies into her home every Saturday afternoon for a weekend ice cream parlour. But eventually, even these activities gradually disappeared.

As the Alzheimer's progressed, Ellen's letters, to my surprise, began to acknowledge the disease and allow me to glimpse the fear she was experiencing as her mind slipped away. I was still living away from home, and her communications betrayed small but significant changes: her frustration that she couldn't remember what used to come naturally (looking up words in her well-worn dictionary, for example) or write her name in her characteristic script.

My most dear Lisabeth, I just got your letter and I feel just like you—it seems

decades since I last saw you. I hope you'll come home before my altzeimers (sp?) gets worse and I don't recognise you anymore. (No joke, it's getting worse!) I hope you'll still love me then.

Are you still subsisting? I am barely subsisting with this horrid weather. It's supposed to turn back to normal (normal? What is normal? For that matter, what is truth?)

Later on, she gave me a window into how she sensed her growing inability to communicate with her caregivers.

I often DON'T understand right and am known to give out false information. For that reason, whatever I say is taken with some degree of scepticism and knowing looks. They try to hide it but I can tell. They think I can't see because they bend over and cover their mouths. I PRETEND not to see. But it hurts. After all, these are people I love and I think they 'love' me. At least, that's what they say. But I have my doubts. Sometimes I do wonder, like when I'm in the middle of saying something that I truly think is important and notice that they start conversations WHILE I AM STILL TALKING. Well, I can't blame them. The kind of things they say to each other must carry more weight. But I've grown used to talking to thin air. Everybody is very polite and they LOOK as if they're listening but I can see from their yawns that their thoughts are far away. Again, it hurts. Lisi, I have to ask you a question, and you must tell me the truth. Is it like that with you?? Are you just being polite when you seem to be listening? If so, I'll

subsist. (Is that the right word, subsist?) Are you yawning even as you read this letter?

I don't think I answered her questions in so many words, but I can say with assurance that I wasn't just being considerate. Our bond transcended the limited conversation she could still muster.

Nevertheless, I'm equally sure I couldn't have always said that. Ours was not a friendship that either of us would necessarily have sought after; in a way, we were both drawn into it by the structure of our Bruderhof life. For one, we had proximity and trust – because she and Ullu and my parents had chosen to dedicate their lives to living in Christian community, our relationship budded in the intimacy that comes of sharing a fridge. The other thing we were able to share was time. In return for the practical services I provided to her, she passed on to me some of her hard-won – so very hard-won – knowledge of life. For me, Ellen wasn't a mentor but an example and a true friend. I learned from her about essential humanness, dignity and the capacity to endure pain and transform it into faithful love.

Everyone comes across chances in life that can bring people together, and many encounters that could be the beginning of a friendship. Still, bonds like ours are increasingly rare. It seems that our society continues to waste tremendous wisdom by limiting intergenerational relationships. A 2016 study of 25 European countries reveals that young adults with friends over the age of 70 and older adults with friends under the age of 30 are minority groups within their respective age categories, and only 18% of the young and 31% of the old report two or more cross-age

friendships. Findings from the United States show that young adults are more likely to live in age-homogenous accommodation than are the old, a tendency that has increased in recent years. How many friendships like the one I had with Ellen never happened because of this pattern?

'I have called you friends', Jesus tells his disciples (John 15:15). Friendship is one of the most gracious of the Creator's gifts, as C S Lewis famously said (and Ellen would have been so proud of me for quoting) – it 'is unnecessary, like philosophy, like art, like the universe itself...It has no survival value; rather it is one of those things thatgive value to survival.' Like all gifts, we have to be prepared to accept and use it.

THE LAST LETTER I RECEIVED FROM ELLEN was in 2014, when I (now married to the Mr Darcy whom she had foretold) moved back to the community where she lived. During her last years, we were once again neighbours, although no longer next door. Ullu had passed away and she was living with her oldest son and his wife. By now, Ellen was transported around the community in a wheelchair, rarely speaking, a faraway look in her eyes. We still spent evenings together, but gone were the discussions of books and the clink of Rummikub tiles. In a way, we were now strangers to each other.

If you search the word 'Alzheimer's' on YouTube, you'll find numerous videos of people who are 'wakened' by a familiar experience or presence – a ballerina hearing music and dancing again, a vacant-faced man suddenly able to recognise his daughter when she replicates an activity they had enjoyed together. The faces come into focus, there are smiles of unearthly beauty and love as recognition returns. Watching such scenes, I think back to Ellen's favourite passage from Dostoyevsky, where he points out the destructiveness of human isolation and how it is only by living together and supporting each other that we can 'draw men's souls out of their solitude' and 'keep the great banner flying'. Even though Alzheimer's had isolated Ellen and taken from her the original expressions of our friendship, our shared commitment to a life of faith kept us connected to the end.

So on that beautiful June morning, when I brought my baby to her bedside five days before she died, Ellen gave us such a moment of 'wakening'. Her eyes opened, a smile filled her face: 'You're here!' She was not gone. She had been there all along. And even after her dying, she is still there – at home in the Great Idea.

So, you dear vile wretch, you try hard to make it through the day and I'll do the same here. Some days are harder than others. It can only get better. The day when I can give you another bear hug will be a better day. I can't wait. But until then, here's a big hug by overseas mail. ELLEN (I can't write in CURSIVE anymore). ⤳

Edvard Munch, *Moonlight on the Shore*, oil on canvas, 1892

Zeal

Oh, to imagine I'm shielding You, when You're
secure as a chant in a red hymnal,
hope of our eyes. You step away on sure
voices, in a child's throat made for canticle.

Oh, to dream I'm some ardent sentinel
bearing the moon on my watch, between a church
and a fire, when it's You who lifts the torch,
clears the tares, so that we might see the stones

pointing home. You pick Your way through the scorch,
calling stragglers—   Oh, those dallying bones.

SOFIA M. STARNES

The Dust on All the Faces

In south Madagascar,
farming families battle to
survive a lethal drought
caused by climate change.

NAVID KERMANI

THERE IS THE DUST on all the faces because there is not enough water even to slake the people's thirst. Cooking, too, is more important than washing: cassava or rice with boiled sweet-potato leaves; the sweet potatoes themselves are all gone. There are the red lips, as if from lipstick, where cactus fruits have become the staple.

Yes, there are the children's distended bellies and the men's thin legs. Where there is still livestock, there are the ox carts hauling mounds of yellow canisters from village to village, each canister holding 20 litres of water. There are the prices of the canisters, which cost more the farther the water has been hauled. But where the way to water is particularly long, most of the oxen are already sold or dead. Then you see whole columns of thin, bowed figures, carrying poles on their necks with a canister at each end. From the source to the consumer we have logged five, seven, even fifteen kilometres on the odometer of our pickup. Where do you get the strength? we ask one of them. He sets his 40 kilos on the ground and answers: he

has a wife and children. From love, then, I think, and I know that that is much too romantic. Where then? It must be more elementary than love.

Are you angry with him? I ask a woman whose husband said he was going to look for work elsewhere because the soil didn't yield crops anymore. He never got in touch again. Now she lives with three children in a refugee camp near the market in the city of Ambovombe. 'Camp' sounds as if there is something. In fact there is the parking lot for the ox carts, around which 70 households have pitched their tents. Tents? Nothing but a couple of poles draped at waist height with plastic sheeting from used rice sacks. When there is no market, the children play football in the square. Many of the

---

Navid Kermani is a German writer born to Iranian immigrants; he lives in Cologne. He has won numerous prizes for his literary and academic work, including the Peace Prize of the German Publishers and Booksellers Association.

Previous spread: A boy sits next to a well in the village of Ambory. All photographs were taken by Alkis Konstantinidis in Madagascar's Androy region in February 2022.

Photography by Alkis Konstantinidis. Used by permission.

children are sick, though: coughs, headaches, diarrhoea or rashes. No wonder, living on a paddock.

No, I am not angry with him, the woman answers; if he loved me, I would show him my anger, but as it is I don't waste any time on him. Collecting wood every day with the children, selling it at the market and buying my mother something to eat – she is too old to go with us to the woods – I don't have the strength to be angry. Her income: 1,000 to 3,000 ariary a day, the equivalent of 25 to 75 pence. That is enough for a little bit of noodles or a little bit of rice with practically nothing else. At least there is a water tap here, just one for 70 households and the livestock, and the owner of the lot is a generous man. Sometimes he gives the refugees some food or brings medicine for the children. Twice a year some organisation brings a few sacks of rice. Most of the aid organisations that hurried to southern Madagascar in autumn 2021, after the United Nations declared the world's first climate-caused famine, have since cut back their work or moved it to the eastern coast, where a series of cyclones came through in February 2022. And the drought threatens to cause famines throughout eastern Africa this autumn, while the available aid money has not increased – although every sack of rice and every ladle of beans has risen in price by one fourth since the outbreak of the European war, which is as far off to the people here as the wars in Yemen or in Ethiopia are to Westerners. And before Russia's attack on Ukraine, the pandemic had already plunged the economy into a severe crisis, while no one had reserves to draw on, not the state and certainly not the people of one of the poorest countries in the world. And in front of the next tent, immobile, sits a frail older man who also tells us his story:

He took out a loan to buy seed, then the crop

A woman holds part of a dead maize plant in a field covered with red sand in Anjeky Beanatara.

failed, and so he had to sell his livestock. When the crops failed for the fifth time in a row, he sold his land too and sought his fortune in the city; that was two years ago. Since then, two more harvests have failed in southern Madagascar, normally a fertile country. His wife died before they reached the camp; he misses her very much, he says. The two children who still live with him collect wood in the forest. He himself worked carrying water, but now he is too weak for it. On market days he begs and gets a few ariary or some food. When all the children have gone, if not before, he will stop begging. Then he'll just stay sitting in front of his tent.

There are the forests that are disappearing; there are the many tree stumps along the wayside, vast areas where there is nothing but stumps left standing. Besides the water canisters, what you see most along the tracks and in the markets are the charcoal sacks. What else are you going to use to cook your rice if there is no electric grid even in the towns, no gas, no running water, no asphalt as far as the eye can see? At a little stand with charcoal sacks we stop. To the right of the track is a nature preserve, which makes us realise what it must have looked like to the left of the track just a few years ago: green with the leaves and the plants spreading between the tree trunks. Now we see to the left a wood that consists more of brown gaps than of trees. A tiny hut with a window-sized hatch through which business is transacted, a back room, and in this tiny building live more than 20 people, we learn to our amazement. Now they all look at us expectantly, from the door, from the window, from in front of the hut, evidently just as amazed as we are. For nine years they've been selling charcoal, and by now that is their sole source of income, because they have

Felix Fitiavantsoa, age 20, and his brother start a fire in a wooded area in order to start cultivating it.

harvested practically nothing in the past seven years. How much does a sack cost? The equivalent of £1.57, although actually they haven't sold any in the last month because the charcoal is cheaper further east, where there is still more forest. Next month, they hope, the price will go up again there; all it needs is for something to happen. What's supposed to happen? I ask. After the cyclones in February, they were able to charge over three dollars a sack; those won't have been the last cyclones. And what happens when all their land is deforested? I won't cut down more than half, says the father, so something will be left for the children. And when your children have cut down the other half, what then? Then I won't be around anymore. Have you never thought about cutting only as many trees as you can replant? No, we haven't got the money for saplings. When we sell a sack, we spend all the money on rice.

I wonder that the nature preserve across the road still seems to be untouched. And their own woods, aren't they also threatened? How do they protect them from wood thieves, who must exist, considering the poverty? No, not here, says the father; to us the woods are sacred; we have learned that from our ancestors. People who cut down someone else's trees will have bad luck. So they cut down only their own future.

There is our shame. Have you any idea why it doesn't rain? I ask. No, that must be God's will, the charcoal-seller answers; neither he nor anyone else among the thirsty people has ever heard the term 'climate change'. And I stand before them, from one of the countries that produces the most greenhouse-gas emissions, while Madagascar's contribution is just 0.01%. They know even less about colonialism, which marked the beginning of the exploitation of nature in Madagascar, as elsewhere. The war in Ukraine, which has made so many foods prohibitively expensive, is also unknown to them. It is almost a consolation that Covid too is very far away. That word they have heard, and they say: at least that disease is only

found in the cities. The fact that tourism has collapsed, and with it the state's revenues – that is not noticeable either in southern Madagascar. Even before the pandemic, the state invested hardly anything in the south, not in the past 30, 40 years. There is an elite that has taken over the colonial rulers' looting. Actually Madagascar would be a rich country: it has vanilla, minerals, gold, sapphires; it has fantastic national parks, endless beaches, some of the greatest biodiversity in the world. As recently as the late 1960s the people were full of hope; the educational system, the infrastructure, the gross domestic product, the arts were developing quite well for postcolonial conditions, but that was before most of the mineral resources had been discovered.

There are the bridges that have become redundant because the river has run dry or is just a trickle in which the people bathe, wash clothes, water the livestock, wash a truck, refill the yellow canisters. When you look at the scene from above, the wide, dry riverbed of brownish-yellow sand looks like a painting by Hieronymus Bosch, composed of countless little vignettes. Not all of them are scenes of hell; it is beautiful to see the children splashing in the water. And how dignified the people are as they wash themselves, men and women, when there is no privacy to be had; their genitals always covered with one hand, their backs always turned to one another.

There are the fields that have been planted: sweet potatoes, beans, scallions, cassava. The cyclones that devastated the east coast seemed a blessing to the south because they finally brought

Navid Kermani, *left*, and the reporting team: Robert Manantena (local guide), Lova Andrianaivomanana (interpreter) and Florien Anjarasoa (driver).

rain, a lot of rain. Those who could still afford seed planted their fields. And, yes, in many fields you can see that something is growing, if meagerly. If it doesn't rain before autumn, it will all die again. There are parents who remember how, when they were children, they ate their fill every day.

We talk with a family that has more land than others. How much exactly? The father stretches out his arm and moves it from left to right. None of it inherited. Their vigour, their perspicacity, their love for their profession too shine in his and in his wife's eyes, which even at their advanced age have a graceful beauty. The family's hut is made of corrugated iron, not of wood like the others, and is painted red and green. The children go to school;

In Madagascar, the ancestors are not dead; they are as present as this table, this neighbour, this tree.

---

three of them have already finished secondary school. I may be mistaken, but I think I see their prosperity not only in the orderliness in the hut, the plastic chairs, the clean dishes on the shelves, the suitcases stacked carefully against the walls. No, I think I also see that they are better off by the couple's tender looks and loving touches. Among the very poor I have not observed any tenderness between adults. But now this family's livelihood too is crumbling, or is already half destroyed. The next source of water is 20 kilometres away; a canister costs 2,000 ariary; it is brought by ox cart. They need two of them every day, and then they still haven't bought any food. How are they supposed to pay for it all, and the school fees besides, and the upkeep for the children at university? In their region, not quite at the epicentre of the drought, the last harvest was four years ago now. They have been drawing on their savings for a long time already, and working their big fields all by

themselves. They could give up their land and move to the city; they still have the means to do so without ending up in a tent camp; they have relatives there who would take them in until they have made a new start. Why are they still here? It is the land of our ancestors, is the answer, as I expected.

The ancestors, one quickly learns in Madagascar, the ancestors are not dead; they are as present as this table, this neighbour, this tree. And, with the ancestors, the afterlife. The only concrete buildings we see along the track are tombs, and sometimes we discover a whole village living in the middle of the fields for a couple of weeks to build one of these complexes together. The only feasts we encounter are funerals, but only when someone has died in old age, that is, at 50, 60 years. Then, yes, then the people dance, drink and laugh. I believe that offers a great deal of reassurance with which to bear the conditions of the present: when it is only the lesser part of reality anyway. So far, the people who flee their villages are comparatively few, and when we asked those in the ox-cart parking lot, all of them talked about going back to be with their ancestors as soon as the sky sends rain again. At most, individual family members go away to earn some money that they can share with those who stay where the ancestors are.

We reach the heart of darkness some two hundred kilometres, or a day's journey with the four-wheel-drive pickup, from Ambovombe, which has a little airport for United Nations aid flights. That is no doubt why all the aid organisations are concentrated there, and when politicians come, they visit the nearby villages; what they see there is shocking enough. A day later, west of the town of Ampanihy to be exact, we see hardly any of the white Jeeps. There are children who no longer play, children who have lost even their imaginations, children who are not curious about the strangers. There is a teacher who asks his pupils to write something on the chalkboard, because we are surprised to hear that they can read and write, one sentence at least. A girl, seven,

eight years old, stands up and slowly writes: *Kememoho.* I realise that it means something terrible by the shocked looks of the others before they translate the sentence for me: 'I am hungry.'

There are villages, whole villages, that come to meet us as soon as we open the doors of the pickup. At first I think the inhabitants are begging for food or money when they surround us, but I soon realise that they aren't familiar with people distributing aid, or at least they aren't expecting it. We sit in a circle in the middle of the village and listen. They are also unaccustomed, I gradually become aware, to talking about their situation, giving voice to their hearts. But there comes a point, and it would probably come anywhere in the world, at which they speak out spontaneously: when I ask who has lost a child to starvation. In one village, three speak up; in another, fifteen; or they answer that it will happen this autumn at the latest if the rain doesn't come. I look at the children's dull eyes, their swollen bellies, the snot on their upper lips because their noses are running constantly, and I don't have to be a doctor to know that the fear is all too justified. One of these children who are now staring at me motionlessly will die then, or two or three or still more.

There is the story that, strangely, always sounds similar when a child starves to death, and it is quite different from how I had imagined it: the child is not lying down, but sitting upright on the ground, their hands around their knees. Then suddenly the potbelly drops, really, so that from the side you can see it fall, and then the child falls over all at once. If it is daytime, the parents are usually in the bush looking for food, which here consists mostly just of cactus leaves and cactus fruits. Someone is sent to fetch them, but doesn't tell them right away that their child is dead. The

A truck parked on the dry bed of the Manambovo River in Tsihombe.

shock, we are told every time, the shock would be too great. Something has happened, they call to the parents from a distance, come quickly. But I knew right away what had happened, says one of the fathers, who ran back to the village.

Some places, there is music, which is glad tidings. With the drought, the culture dies out too; there was nothing besides agriculture and feasts before, and without the one, no one has money for the other. Southern Madagascar is famous for its musicians, but we ask about them in vain. And so it transfixes us like a choir of angels when, on the drive to the coast, we discover a big, yes, almost a huge crowd on a village square, and through the open windows a tinny electric guitar, like a sound out of a Detroit garage, and a breathless beat blow in. Funeral! cries one of my companions, and the other adds, If there is music, you know that we're back up to the minimum subsistence level.

We get out and make our way through to a pickup truck with two huge loudspeakers mounted above its covered bed. On the bed of the truck are a drummer, a singer and an ultra-cool man playing security guard. Next to the truck is a diesel generator, its noise being drowned out by the music. But where is the electric guitar coming from? We go around the truck and find the young rhythm guitarist sitting next to the driver, and alone in the back seat the aged band leader, playing wild solos while nevertheless nodding at us as nonchalantly as Keith Richards. Red baseball cap, dark sunglasses, Hawaiian shirt and moustache trimmed thin. The crowd – men, women, old people, children – dance ecstatically, some even spilling their expensive beer. It is the proximity to the sea, we learn, that provides the village with food, a little income and, because of the income, music.

There is the realisation of how little human

Local boys give drinking water to their herd of zebu cattle on a beach in Faux Cap.

beings really need: only soil, a wood, a lake, a river or a sea that offers them enough food; after that the superfluous begins, the impractical, the beautiful, making their lives rich. There is the water that the children spray at each other because there is enough of it. There is the perplexity because humanity has more than an abundance of all goods, but distributes them so inadequately. Madagascar itself has enough of everything, but it also has a government that spends 95% of its revenue in the capital because it has perpetuated the centralisation of the colonial rulers and only survives thanks to Western aid. There would have to be roads, electricity, wells, water pipelines to distribute the goods that there are, if the rain won't fall. Instead the world community, meaning only the rich countries of course, distributes some money and a few sacks of rice to avoid having to see pictures of starvation and death. And where nothing is distributed, no one is looking anyway. Nonetheless, the question remains, nowhere as dramatically as in southern Madagascar perhaps, why the modern age, of all eras, doesn't seem to have heard of the future.

On the beach of the tiny coastal town of Beheloka, we meet the fisherman Christophe Germain Mananandroko, sitting between two canoes. Strong build, balding with white hair cut short, a white jersey with the sleeves cut off and the French football association's FFF logo, *Fédération Française de Football*, which coincidentally is the abbreviation of the climate-action organisation *Fridays For Future*. And in fact Christophe, who has some schooling and an old, small smartphone, has heard quite a bit about climate change and knows that the drought very probably has to do with it. But – only the drought? About the same time as the drought began, the wind became much stronger, so that Christophe can only go out fishing twice a week on average, and when he notices that the wind is coming up, he rows back to shore straight away. But many of his younger colleagues are first-generation fishermen and

don't know the warning signs. Just three months ago, two of them didn't come home from the sea, on the same night. But the sea, the sea – even if the wind doesn't blow, it's no longer the sea he knows. Christophe remembers perfectly: when he was young, 10, 15 years old, he only had to stand knee-deep in the water, and hundreds, thousands of fish flurried around his legs. Catching five kilos took no time at all. Now you go out in the water, Christophe says, and you don't see any fish at all, not one. Even beyond the reef there aren't many left. The night before last he was out with his son, bright moon and calm sea, put out at eight, back

---

Christophe remembers perfectly: when he was young, he only had to stand knee-deep in the water, and hundreds, thousands of fish flurried around his legs.

---

at four, and what did they catch? One and a half kilos, barely enough for lunch for the big family. It used to be that he could put something aside, buy the children a few presents: not anymore; the grandchildren don't get any.

Is it because of the industrial fishing? I ask. Yes, there are big Japanese ships out there; they have a treaty with the state. But they've been around a long time; the industrial ships can't be the only reason. So maybe the depletion of the fish is connected with the wind? And the wind with climate change? I don't know, Christophe answers, but our main problem is a different one anyway. What is it? Our main problem is that the coral reef is almost completely destroyed now, and we did that ourselves. The reef is the fishes' home; they all throng there; every fisherman knows that. We have one of the longest coral reefs in the Indian Ocean, and now there is hardly anything to be caught there; we have to go farther and farther out to sea to catch anything at all, but out there there's the problem of the waves; our boats aren't made for that.

Is there no one who explains the connections to the fishermen?

There are programmes to raise the fishermen's awareness, by the World Wildlife Fund (WWF), by Blue Ventures, by the Madagascar National Parks organisation, but they only explain what the fishermen already know, Christophe says: that's nothing new; the fishermen already know their lives depend on the reef.

Then why are they destroying it? I ask. Why are they destroying their own future?

There is a new generation, Christophe answers; there are more and more people living in the villages, and more and more of them go to sea because their land doesn't yield crops anymore. They come from the whole inland region now to catch fish, but they don't know how it's done. Cast their nets over the reef; fix them to the reef; anchor on the reef; they even walk on the reef; no one used to do any of that before.

Before when?

When I was young, let's say 40 years ago, no fisherman ever so much as touched the reef. We didn't need any WWF; our ancestors forbade us.

And why have the people lost their relationship to the sea?

Greed, Christophe answers straight away, it is greed. Then he tells us of one of the fishermen in the village who has bought special nets to catch more fish, which in turn gets him more money. Of the little that is still there, this man, a neighbour, catches everything and doesn't even leave the others what's left. This greed for more and more, we never knew that before, no one among us; we were all more or less equal.

How do you see the future of fishing?

Bad, very bad; it will disappear here completely, I'm afraid.

Don't the programmes have any effect at all?

Nonsense. At the training the people say,

'Yes, yes', and the next day they carry on as they have been.

Then the cause is in the people themselves?

Yes, we're to blame, we ourselves; we know it and do it anyway. The cause is: the people's minds are sinking lower.

But the people can't help climate change, they can't help that it doesn't rain; that the wind has grown so strong.

Yes, I know, they can't help that.

What do you think, then, why is it, I ask, human beings are so clever, just take this smartphone here – mine – there's so much intelligence in it, in such a tiny device, so much inventiveness, cunning, technical skill. So why are human beings destroying the Earth, although their lives depend on it?

Christophe laughs sadly and says nothing.

Have you really no idea? I insist. I don't know, myself; I've come all this way, from far Germany to here, and I haven't found any answer.

Christophe takes my smartphone from my hand – it is newer and bigger than his – and he says, look, this device, this has a huge memory. Thirty gigabytes, a hundred gigabytes, two hundred gigabytes?

I am surprised that an old fisherman in a tiny, remote village on the south coast of Madagascar, several days' journey from the nearest asphalt road – that this man knows the word 'gigabyte'. And at the same time I am not surprised, after having heard sharp guitar riffs and racing beats in a still more remote village.

In this smartphone alone, Christophe continues, there is so much more memory than any human being has. But this memory is nothing compared to the memory of nature. The memory of nature goes back much further; it goes back to the beginning of the world's creation.

There is also the fisherman Christophe Germain Mananandroko, who seems to know more than we do. ⤜

Originally published in *Die Zeit* no 39, 2022. Translated from the German by Tony Crawford. Used by permission.

Aleksey Savrasov, *Winter Road*, oil on canvas, ca. 1870

Winter

Here it is, my dearest winter,
dearer than the fall or spring.
Here it is, my native country,
where I'm always wintering.

Here are soldiers, soft as cotton,
but in khaki head to toe.
I'm to blame for their misfortune,
don't allow them in my home—

which is why they're running, running
all across our hard-white land,
like they'll run along that shoreline
where their days will one day end.

JULIA NEMIROVSKAYA

Translated from the Russian by Boris Dralyuk.

Caravaggio, *Crucifixion of Saint Peter*, oil on canvas, 1601

Christian Strangeness

A podcasting scholar sums up the history of pain in two artworks and the lives of three illustrious women.

TOM HOLLAND

In this interview, **Plough's** *Peter Mommsen speaks with Tom Holland, the historian, cricket fan and podcaster, about how Christianity changed humanity's view of suffering.*

Peter Mommsen: Since our topic is so vast, you and I have agreed to structure our conversation about the history of pain by picking a sculpture, a painting and three famous figures from history. Let's start with the artworks. One is the Greco-Roman sculpture of Laocoön and the other is Caravaggio's *Crucifixion of Saint Peter.* The first is pagan, while the second is obviously Christian. What happened between the two of these?

Tom Holland: The statue of Laocoön tells a story that appears in Virgil's *Aeneid* and is set in the Trojan War. The Greeks have left this strange horse and the Trojans think, 'Let's take it inside the walls of Troy.' Laocoön hurls a spear at the side of the horse and there's a clanging sound, suggesting, perhaps, that there are men in armour inside it.

At that moment, snakes appear from the sea and crush Laocoön in their coils. This seems to the Trojans a marker that by striking the horse, Laocoön has committed an offence against the gods. But in fact, they are crushing him for a quite different offence. The result of this confusion is the annihilation of Troy. What you get there is the sense that mortals are the playthings of the gods and often the gods take pleasure in destroying humans. It's what Shakespeare articulates many centuries later in *King Lear:* 'As flies to wanton boys

---

Tom Holland lives in London and is an award-winning historian, biographer and broadcaster. He is the author of many books, most recently Dominion. *He cohosts* The Rest Is History *podcast and is a regular contributor to the* Guardian, *the* Times of London, *the* Wall Street Journal *and the* New York Times.

are we to the gods / they kill us for their sport.'

By contrast, the Caravaggio shows the crucifixion of Peter. What is expressive of a radical change from the classical period is that the humiliation implicit in a crucifixion has been transmuted – Peter is the hero of this painting. He isn't being mocked by the gods; he isn't a creature whose hopes have been dashed by fate. Because of course we know that Peter will emerge as the rock on which Christ's church is built and that his heirs will succeed the Caesars as the masters of Rome and stand at the head of the Christian church.

Why would a humiliated hero have seemed foreign to the creators of the Laocoön?

For the Greeks and Romans, the ability to withstand excruciating pain was the measure of a man. The classic example is Mucius Scaevola, who according to the historian Livy infiltrates the enemy camp, is captured, is told to reveal what he knows and, as a mark of his contempt for that demand, thrusts his hand into the fire until it's consumed without once letting out a hint of pain. This is the kind of story the Romans adored. The pain endured by a hero becomes the measure of a hero.

Conversely, the pain suffered by, say, a slave who is nailed to a cross is contemptible. There is elevated pain and there is servile pain. The servile pain is to be mocked and despised.

So by definition, the victim of a crucifixion can't be heroic?

The whole point of crucifixion is to humiliate and degrade. It is the punishment seen as paradigmatically suited to a rebellious slave. Not only is it excruciatingly painful and protracted – you could survive on the cross for days – but it's also public. You are hung up there like a piece of meat and your sufferings are objects of public ridicule. There's nothing you can do to brush away the birds who might peck out your eyes or attack your genitals. You can't stop people from watching your gasps and heaving breath as you struggle to lift yourself up to gulp for air. It's this that makes you serve as a billboard of Roman power.

This is the penalty that is visited on rebels against Roman rule out in the provinces and so it becomes the fate suffered by Jesus. The *titulus*, the board affixed above his head by Pilate's orders, says that he is the king of the Jews. And there can be no king of the Jews in a Roman province.

The Romans themselves were hesitant to speak about the realities of crucifixion. Why?

They found it sordid. They felt that it was beneath them to represent it in art, even to write about it. Josephus describes how Titus, the Roman general, had his soldiers crucify vast numbers of captives before the walls of Jerusalem. But he doesn't describe what it was like to be sentenced to that, what the process is, how long you might spend on the cross, what happens to the body once the person is dead. It's only in the Gospels that we get that. And the Gospel writers, of course, are not writing as Romans.

Even for them, though, the cross was still a 'scandal' in a powerfully visceral way.

Saint Paul says it's a stumbling block to the Jews, but to everyone else – to the Greeks, to the Romans – it's a scandal. For Paul, the fact that Jesus was crucified lies at the heart of Jesus' mission and of how he relates to God's plan. That's why everything – the very character of the world, of God, of God's relationship to humanity – has been upended by this. It is the most shocking thing imaginable.

Into the second and third centuries, Christian writers seem embarrassed to talk about the crucifixion. For critics of Christianity, both pagan and Jewish, the manner of Jesus' death becomes an attack point that they return to again and again. Even once Constantine has converted and the Roman Empire starts to become largely Christian, there is a reluctance to portray Jesus on the cross.

Laocoön and His Sons, likely 27 BC to AD 68, Museo Pio Clementino, Rome

One of the earliest such portrayals by a Christian is an ivory in the British Museum that was done in the early fifth century, a century after Constantine's conversion. It shows Jesus as an athlete. He's nailed to the cross, but he's looking unbelievably buff, and he's wearing the loincloth of an Olympic victor. His expression is calm and dignified. That's a tradition that persists throughout the centuries, certainly in the Orthodox world, up to the present. There's a reluctance to dwell on the agonies, the horrors, the suffering, the full ordeal.

Yet at the same time, from the beginning Christ's suffering becomes a pattern for the suffering of the martyrs: suffering as an *imitatio Christi*, an imitation of Christ. As Paul says, without the example of Christ, without the fact that he rose from the dead, it would all be madness without significance; suffering would simply be suffering. But because Christ has provided this model of triumph over suffering, those who follow him can share in it.

At the back of any portrayal of the saints, including Caravaggio's, is always the image of Christ on the cross. Caravaggio paints Saint Peter as an old man, clearly suffering. He's not an athlete as in the fifth-century ivory crucifix; he's not a figure of dignity. That stands in the line of the portrayal of Christ that emerges in Latin Christendom. Around the year 1000, you start to get portrayals of Christ in his full suffering on the cross. Over the centuries that follow, the emphasis on Christ's sufferings becomes more and more intense and so does the sense of identification that Christians feel with those sufferings.

There's a second-century record of martyrs who were thrown into the arena in Lyon. One is a woman of noble birth, but we're not told her name. Instead, we're told the name of one of her slaves, Blandina. Blandina suffers terribly in the arena and the author tells us that she dies resembling Christ on the cross. That's a paradigmatic insight into the way the Christian understanding of the crucifixion upends the social and gender norms that had prevailed in the Roman Empire. Blandina, a female slave, is compared to Christ when her mistress and the men in the arena are not.

As a martyr, the early Christians believed, Blandina wouldn't have to wait for the Day of Judgement to enter the palace of heaven. Instead, this female slave would be escorted straight to the inner sanctum of the palace of God and be seated by God's side ahead of everybody else.

That's the radical potential that Christians see in suffering for those who are prepared to consecrate their suffering to Christ. The aftershocks of that endure to this day. They explain what is strange about Caravaggio's painting. This is a radical reconfiguring of the meaning of suffering for humanity. 'The last shall be first.'

Not a sentiment that would have occurred to an ancient Spartan or Roman.

Julius Caesar is said to have slaughtered a million Gauls and enslaved another million, and not only did he not feel bad about this, he regarded it as the measure of his greatness. Likewise, Leonidas of Sparta, who died at Thermopylae as portrayed in the film *300*, was king in a city that depended on a vast population of slaves. He had no qualms about this. He thought it was the order of the world. The Spartans had annexed this neighbouring city, turned the population into slaves and bred them to be as placid and servile as possible. They would kill any of them who seemed too uppity.

To us, the Third Reich is the absolute embodiment of evil, perhaps in a way that Sparta isn't. I think that is because the Third Reich stands in the context of a Christian civilisation for whom contempt for the suffering of others is seen as an offence against our shared humanity. The Spartans didn't have that context and that may be why we judge them less harshly than we judge the Nazis.

The Christian view has had its critics, of course. Friedrich Nietzsche famously referred to it as contemptible, as 'slave morality'.

He refers to the 'blond beast' being gelded by Christianity. The idea that Christianity neutered the pagan virtues of heroism and strength and power, and indeed cruelty, was hugely influential on the Nazis. Fascism was a conscious attempt to roll back the centuries of Christian history and return to the primal ferocity and emphasis on glory and power that the fascists saw the Greeks and Romans embodying, while simultaneously embracing everything that was modern and new and gleaming – planes, tanks, jets, whatever. That fusion of the pre-Christian and the post-Christian enabled those who signed up to fascist ideals to commit the atrocities that they did.

But it's important to acknowledge that Christians themselves have been capable of committing appalling atrocities. Christians worship a God who suffered horribly on an instrument of torture, but that has not prevented them from inflicting sufferings on others. That is the great paradox of Christian history.

Take for example the Inquisition's persecution of the heretics we call 'Cathars' in 13th-century France. The idea of denying people freedom of conscience strikes us moderns as monstrous and appalling. But the story is slightly more complicated, because the inquisitors make inordinate efforts to persuade the people to see the error of their ways. They don't want to condemn the people they are investigating to the flames. To burn a heretic is a mark of failure.

There's an interesting contrast to the atrocities that were committed in much the same region several centuries later in the wake of the French Revolution, when the revolutionary armies moved into the outer reaches of France. Because the French Revolution is consciously setting itself against Christianity, the sense that every human being is created in the image of God and has to be treated potentially as an image of Christ is gone. It's the same in the 20th century when the Communists in Russia and China launch their mass killing campaigns. They were wholly without such inhibitions because they lacked the framing that Christianity had provided. Even though they were driven by a Christian kind of motive – the

Matthias Grünewald, *Saint Elizabeth of Hungary*,
grisaille on wood, 1511

The martyrdom of Blandina, illustration by Jan
Luyken in *Martyrs Mirror*, 1685

Cecil Beaton, *A Coronation Portrait
of Queen Elizabeth II*, 1953

desire to uplift the poor, the suffering, the weak, and to cast down the strong – the fact that the revolutionaries discarded doctrinal Christianity enabled them to act with a degree of brutality that even the Inquisition at its worst was reluctant to do.

Today the Inquisition and the Crusades are constantly held up as examples of the brutality of which Christianity is capable. But of course, the standards by which we condemn them are themselves Christian.

We started with artwork, now let's turn to three figures from history who illustrate this Christian insight. You've already mentioned the first one.

Yes, Blandina, the second-century slave girl who died in the arena in Lyon. She always strikes me as such a fascinating figure right at the start of the Christian story – to her fellow believers, the nobility that her suffering brought her redeems her from her slavery and elevates her to the highest possible rank. That idea is so fundamental to Christian history and it's right there at the beginning.

And it then extends to those born into privilege who don't suffer martyrdom, such as our next example, Elizabeth of Hungary.

So she is of royal birth, living in the early 13th century, about the same time as the Inquisition's persecution of the Cathars. She's motivated by the desire for a kind of identification with Christ that around the same time is also motivating both the Cathars and Saint Francis of Assisi. The yearning to identify with and emulate the sufferings of Christ is sometimes branded by the church as heresy and on other occasions is saluted as the behaviour of saints.

Like Francis, Elizabeth is canonised a saint after her death. Though born into wealth and power, she bears in mind that the first shall be last and so she humbles herself. She works in a hospital, hugging lepers with their sores to her breast, mopping their brows. She feels that she is beckoned by the suffering Christ. That kind of behaviour would've made no sense to anyone before the Christian period.

Elizabeth's actions sound pathological, even insane. Yet she is very clearly, I think, a precursor of all kinds of movements that are current today. For example, she refuses to eat food that comes from her husband's peasantry, that's been extorted from them. If you want to put it that way, she will only eat food that has been ethically sourced.

You can see why, for the medieval authorities, this kind of approach would seem dangerous. It wasn't just the safe and pious path that it may seem to be in hindsight. Others were executed for the same thing.

Our last example is in many ways very different, but shares Elizabeth's name and royal heritage. The late Queen Elizabeth II didn't give away all her wealth or serve in a hospital. But there's something about her life that is explicable only in terms of Christianity, an embrace of – suffering may be the wrong word – but certainly self-abnegation.

It might sound ridiculous to say that the Queen, who was one of the richest people in the world, lived a life of suffering.

We're deliberately being a bit ridiculous here.

Yet it's not actually so far-fetched. If we take the 20th-century existentialists at their word, one of the worst kinds of suffering is boredom. And in that sense, the Queen actually suffered quite a lot, because she led quite a boring life. And she absolutely did so as a Christian. For her, the coronation oaths she took were a sacrament.

Like a vow of religious life?

She'd been anointed by God, and she felt wedded to her role. Every Christmas, she would broadcast a message in Britain. The older she got, the more overtly Christian that message became. I think she was one of the most impressive spokespeople for Christianity in contemporary Britain.

I can imagine all kinds of people snorting at the idea that monarchy is a kind of suffering. But perhaps, to a degree, it is. When she died, I think many people found themselves surprised by how moved they were by the rituals and ceremony of her obsequies. Britain is in some ways an aggressively secular society. But those two weeks between her death and her funeral enabled people in Britain and perhaps beyond to get a sense of the strangeness that the Queen herself was wedded to. And it was a Christian strangeness.

This telephone interview from 31 January 2023 has been edited for clarity and length. To listen to a longer audio version, visit *plough.com/hollandinterview*.

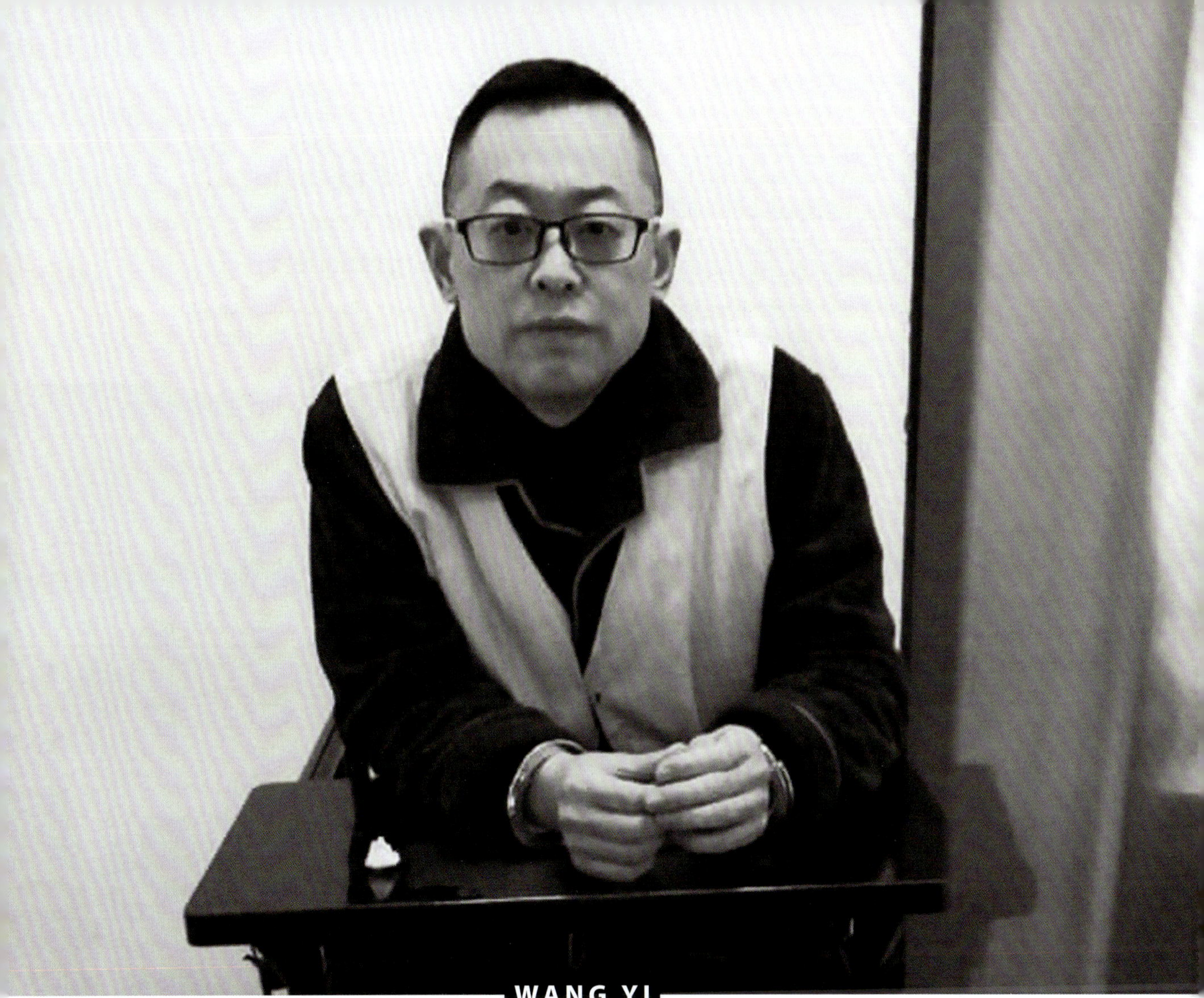

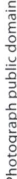

WANG YI

Photograph public domain.

Costly Allegiance

An imprisoned Chinese pastor calls churches to face repression boldly.

Artwork reproduced in L. Perret, *Les Catacombes de Rome* (Paris, 1851).

THE WRITER OF THE FOLLOWING *sits in a Chinese prison. Wang Yi is perhaps China's best-known pastor of a house church since the day in December 2018 when he opened the church door and faced a crowd of officers who arrested both him and his wife, Jiang Rong. Officers also tracked down and arrested the entirety of Early Rain's leadership structure and dismantled the church's social and educational initiatives, which included mental health and foster care programmes and care for the elderly and the families of prisoners.*

Wang Yi's thought and writing have developed over the years since his conversion in 2005; his training as a legal scholar influenced by both Western and Chinese political philosophy goes hand in hand with his development as a theologian and biblical scholar who has shifted his focus increasingly from the topic of rights to the kingdom of God and eschatology.

For Wang Yi and other Chinese Christians these are not ivory-tower matters but immensely practical theology in an unceasingly challenging situation. Wang Yi's work reminds us to consider that all authorities and powers, governing or cultural, are in competition with God the Creator for the highest love and allegiance of humankind. There will be times when maintaining our proper allegiance to King Jesus alone will require of us 'faithful disobedience'. —Hannah Nation

The office of apostle is inseparable from the status of being a prisoner.

PAUL IS A PRISONER who has made an appeal to Caesar for his case. However, Paul has been imprisoned and his case delayed for two whole years; the identity of 'prisoner' clings to him. He is also renting the house where he is imprisoned. This is just like the time during the Cultural Revolution where if you were executed by shooting, you would have to pay for the bullet as well. Paul's prison was not a place where you could eat and sleep for free; prisoners were required to bear the cost of being imprisoned. This was truly unfair. Although Roman law was more civilised than ancient Chinese law, it's uncivilised compared to our modern laws: Paul, at this time, had neither religious nor basic human rights. However, when Paul emphasises the two years in which he was imprisoned, and the consequent boldness with which he preached and the fruitfulness of unhindered ministry, he doesn't define his situation by his suffering. Instead, he sounds like he's describing a type of opportunity. What Paul cares about, and even what the narrator, Luke, is concerned about, is not the way by which they came to Rome, but their purpose for coming there.

The gospel creates a paradox in this situation. As each day passes, and being a prisoner seems more and more like Paul's permanent status, he becomes more and more like an apostle. His physical body is imprisoned, but the gospel is free and unhindered. This is exactly what Paul means when he writes, 'For I think that God has exhibited us apostles as last of all'. The apostles are compared to the prisoners of war who are paraded

---

Wang Yi is a leader of Early Rain Covenant Church, a house church in Chengdu, China. He is currently serving a nine-year prison sentence for refusing to comply with People's Republic of China regulations regarding church registration.

Hannah Nation is the managing director of the Center for House Church Theology and is the editor of Faithful Disobedience: Writings on Church and State from a Chinese House Church Movement, *from which this article is adapted.*

by a triumphant Roman army to highlight the glory of their victory. In this sense, the apostles are captives who reveal the glory of Christ's kingdom. If the gospel implies that this world is enemy-occupied territory, then the office of apostle is inseparable from the status of prisoner.

Source: 'The Mission and Labour Camp of the Gospel', 2013.

The demands of the house churches are, in essence, the demands of the gospel.

IN 1955, WANG MINGDAO WROTE 'We – For the Sake of Faith', which became the Chinese church's statement of defence before kings and society. For decades, house churches in China have defended and sought religious freedom and freedom of conscience for the sake of the gospel. Although it continues to suffer government persecution, the church strives to preach the gospel of Christ and it does not stop worshipping and gathering together. Although it lacks legal status, the church still forms community life for tens of millions of citizens in contemporary China.

People ask, 'Aren't house churches illegal?' I want to answer honestly: yes. For 60 years, house churches have been illegal in terms of church worship, assembly, doctrine, religious property, the sacraments, evangelism, missions, theological training, pastor ordination, publishing, children's Sunday school ministry and charity work. For 60 years, house churches have taken a posture of 'non-violent non-cooperation' to violate all aspects of China's religious management and related legal enforcement. To deny this is to deny the road they have been travelling on and to deny the reality of church–state conflict in China for the last half century.

But here is the more important question: is the Chinese government illegal? We should honestly and courageously respond: yes. For 60 years, this country has continuously trampled upon its own constitution and laws regarding religious freedom. Whether it is church worship, freedom of assembly, doctrine, religious property, the sacraments, missions, seminary training, pastor ordination, publishing, children's Sunday school, charity work and so on, the government uses illegal, autocratic and barbarous methods to oppress the church and the children of Christ in China.

So, again we ask, 'Aren't house churches illegal?' If the Bible is the 'constitution' for Christians and the church, then over the past 60 years the house churches have been the paragon of following God's law and freedom of conscience in Chinese society. I must say that we have not violated the higher, most supreme law (James 2:8). Moreover, precisely because we must observe that law within our hearts, we have not dared *not* to violate the system of religious regulations that deprives and controls the Christian's mission to worship God and preach the gospel.

'Aren't house churches illegal?' If the constitution is 'the king' of the modern state, if the Chinese government claims that its power comes from the Chinese constitution and that it must comply with the constitution, I must honestly answer that for 60 years the house churches have been the perfect model for submitting to the king and following the constitution. The church follows the constitution up to a point, even though all government officials have chosen to defy it, imprisoning those who do not violate the constitution with them. Still, the church continues to act 'according to law' by upholding the constitutional right to worship God and preach the gospel just as before. And because we must abide by a higher 'constitutional power', we dare not comply with

The early Christian symbols in this article are based on paintings and engravings found in Roman catacombs.

the unconstitutional actions of the religious administrative system.

The demands of the house churches are, in essence, the demands of the gospel. This demand is in direct conflict with the state. Article 35 of the constitution guarantees 'freedom of religious belief'. In other words, social transformation, political progress, freedom, democracy, the rule of law, human rights – these are all good things in the eyes of Christians. But they are never the true pursuit of the church. Whether it is slavery or democracy, monarchy or rule of law, the Bible teaches that the church must obey the government's authority. In short, the church of Christ is not at all interested in any political and legal system. However, under any political and legal system the church claims the freedom to worship God and proclaim the gospel.

Therefore, during 60 years of religious persecution, the house churches have continuously adopted peaceful, patient means to become law-abiding representatives of Chinese society. Lord permitting, the church is willing to suffer under any system in order to comply with any unfair and unjust law. However, the one law that the church cannot obey is the law that attempts to deprive and control our worship of God and proclamation of the gospel. In the public sphere, the church must regard these laws as 'unconstitutional'. In terms of our faith, the church must also regard these laws as evil and anti-Christ.

We raise our voice to seek mercy for all of our persecutors.

AS A HOUSE-CHURCH PASTOR, I thank and praise God Almighty for all persecution and restrictions suffered by the church. God foreordains everything according to his good and blameless will. He trains and purifies his church and his children in China. Moreover, he gives us the most unmerited blessing of suffering for righteousness' sake (1 Pet 3:14). In a larger sense and even on a personal level, I actually prefer for persecution to continue. I am also willing to submit to God's will and prepared to endure a more protracted church–state conflict; this would be incomparably better for our spiritual life and for our final hope.

But we raise our voice to seek mercy for all our persecutors. They do not believe in the gospel of Christ, and they do not believe in God's righteous anger and curse. But do we believe the gospel?

We raise our voice because we take pity on those compatriots who cannot have more freedom and more opportunity to hear the gospel. They cannot attend churches because of religious persecution. They do not believe the gospel of Christ, and they do not care about what they have lost. But don't we care?

We raise our voice also due to our frequent weakness under persecution. 'If it be possible, let this cup pass from me; nevertheless, not as I will, but as you will' (Matt 26:39). With year after year of persecution and restrictions, we recognise that Christians often feel cowardly and afraid. They carry anger and bitterness and even in the midst of suffering it is hard to avoid feeling self-righteous and prideful. Therefore, we are not chasing after the hero of religious freedom. We are petitioning the Lord Jesus Christ to keep our generation from temptation and deliver us from evil, lest we are 'so utterly burdened beyond our strength' (2 Cor 1:8) that we dishonour the name of the Lord.

Sixty years ago, the Chinese government terrorised Christians into handing over their names and identities to Caesar. From 1950 to 1954, some 410,000 Christians (approximately 50% of Christians at the time) voluntarily or under duress signed the Three-Self Patriotic Manifesto. They openly betrayed the Lord Jesus Christ and his church; the effect was to withdraw the church from public society.

Sixty years later, the Lord's church needs to call every Christian once again, for the sake of the gospel, to hand over their names and identities. We have a responsibility to use a different call – our appeal and petition, apologetics and signature campaign – to make our own public confession to defend the gospel and the church in the face of those in power. By the blood of Christ, we will wash the Chinese church clean of the Lord's shame.

What we need is not a religious civil rights movement. What we need is a genuine gospel movement. Our action takes place in this currently unprecedented period of urbanisation and social transformation, in which house churches can conduct evangelism trainings, church planting, church transformation and missions work and obey the gospel's cultural mandate. Thus the house churches can more firmly establish church membership, build local churches and form a visible Christian community for the world. We can use the issue of religious freedom to challenge other citizens' consciences, bring forth the courage of church members and call those believers who have drifted away to renew their commitment.

The church does not need to proudly fight the state for our non-existent rights. The church needs to be humble so that this country can be blessed by the benefits of the gospel. We need to request the state to recognise and respect the freedom we already have.

The church also does not at all need or rely on any external 'religious freedom' to maintain and live out the Christian faith. On the contrary, over the past 60 years the church has already lived out a true 'freedom' because of the Christian faith. Therefore, the church's petitions, appeals, apologetics, signature campaign and calls to end religious persecution are not for external benefits for the visible church; rather, they are for the expansion of Christ's kingdom and the blessing of other communities. 'Not only to avoid God's wrath but also for the sake of conscience' (Rom 13:5).

Source: 'Raising Our Voices to End 60 Years of Religious Persecution', 2011.

This article is adapted from Wang Yi, et al, *Faithful Disobedience: Writings on Church and State from a Chinese House Church Movement*, edited by Hannah Nation and J D Tseng (IVP Academic, 2022). Copyright © 2022 by Center for House Church Theology from Urban China. Used by permission.

The Speaking Tree

*In an Anglo-Saxon poem, a tree becomes
the meeting place of horror and joy.*

ELEANOR PARKER

LYING AWAKE ONE NIGHT, alone in the dark while everyone else is sleeping, a man receives a strange vision. He sees a great tree lifted up into the sky, radiant with light, so huge that it seems to fill the whole universe. It is studded with jewels, adorned with gold, with bright banners streaming from its limbs. Watching in awe, the solitary man suddenly has a sense that he is no longer alone: he is surrounded by a vast company of spirits, all gazing in silent adoration upon the mighty tree.

Naturally enough, he is seized with terror at this unearthly vision, but he can't stop looking at the tree. As he gazes at it, he sees more details; he notices that beneath its covering of gold and gems, the tree is bleeding. It seems to flicker as he watches it, as things do in dreams. At one moment he sees it drenched in blood, the next adorned with the finest treasure. Then the tree begins to speak: 'It was long ago – I remember it yet – that I was cut down at the edge of a forest, removed from my root.' At this moment, it becomes clear which particular tree is speaking: the Cross of Christ, 'the Saviour's tree'.

So begins the Anglo-Saxon poem *The Dream of the Rood,* which survives in a 10th-century manuscript from southern England. It tells the story of the Crucifixion as seen through the eyes of the Cross, which speaks in its own words, describing how it was forced to participate in Christ's death. The tree tells how it was violently wrested from its forest home to be made a tool of execution and how it witnessed the suffering of the 'young hero, God almighty' who willingly climbed upon it. The tree loves and admires this warrior, who ascends his cross like a soldier going into battle, but it is forced to become his slayer as Christ endures a terrible and humiliating death.

They suffer together, the Warrior and the Cross.

It's a profoundly intimate bond. Both are driven through with cruel nails; they are pinned together and their bodies mingle sap and sweat, water and blood. Christ bears it all without a word, but in this poem the Cross can give voice to the pain of both, the agony, the fear. Unlike Christ, the Cross has not chosen this death and the pain is almost too much for it to bear; it is, after all, only an ordinary

> **Unlike Christ, the Cross has not chosen this death, and the pain is almost too much for it to bear; it is, after all, only an ordinary tree.**

tree. But it holds firm to its position, as its Lord has commanded and stands fast until the end.

When the battle is over and the young warrior dead, the Cross feels Christ's body being lifted from its arms and carried away for burial. It doesn't see what happens next, because its part in the story is over. We have to fill in those details for ourselves: the garden, the stone rolled away, the empty tomb. The Cross knows none of this. Its knowledge ends on the evening of Christ's burial, as the grieving disciples depart, singing a song of mourning, their voices dying away. The Cross itself is buried in a deep pit and forgotten, its purpose completed in the eyes of the executioners. Centuries later, though, it tells us, it was rediscovered; like its Lord, it rose from the grave to be exalted and honoured across the world. The poem explains how through Christ's death and resurrection the journey from suffering and grief to glory and joy, that the Cross has experienced, is

Eleanor Parker teaches medieval literature at Brasenose College, Oxford, and is the author of Dragon Lords: The History and Legends of Viking England *(2018) and* Conquered: The Last Children of Anglo-Saxon England *(2022).*

Opposite: Anglo-Saxon cross, Church of Saint Michael, Cropthorne, Worcestershire.

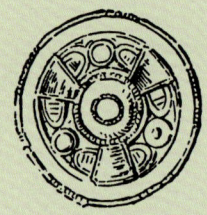

Wondrous was that victory-beam,
and I stained with sins,
wounded with wickedness.
I saw the tree of glory
adorned with drapery,
shining with joys,
decked with gold;
gems worthily wrapped the Ruler's tree.
But through that gold I could perceive
ancient wretches' hostility,
so that it first began
to bleed on the right side.
I was entirely afflicted with sorrow;
I was afraid at the fair vision.

I saw that eager beacon
change its clothing and colour;
at times it was drenched with moisture,
soaked with the flow of sweat;
at times it was adorned with treasure.

But I, lying there a long while,
beheld, sorrowful, the Saviour's tree,
until I heard that it spoke.
The best of trees began to speak words.

From *The Dream of the Rood* (trans Eleanor Parker).

now held out to human beings too: through the Cross, we have been granted a home in the heavens.

That was the message *The Dream of the Rood* was designed to teach its Anglo-Saxon audience. This poem was first written for a culture to which Christianity was still relatively new: a few lines of it appear, carved in runes, on a giant stone cross made in the early eighth century, only a hundred years or so after the Anglo-Saxons began to be converted to Christianity. Though the fuller version as it is preserved today is from a few centuries later, some form of this poem may be among the earliest surviving Christian poems in English.

The story it tells is shaped to resonate with an Anglo-Saxon audience. By imagining Christ as a warrior and the Cross as his loyal follower, it echoes the relationship found in poems like *Beowulf*, where the bond between a warrior and his men is invested with the most intense emotions of love and grief. The opening vision of the Cross as a great tree, towering as tall as the heavens and worshipped by all beings in the world, likely draws on the pre-Christian veneration of sacred trees. It presents the Cross as a kind of world-tree, something like Yggdrasil in Norse mythology, whose branches span the universe and connect the realms of heaven and earth.

The poem is emphatic in describing the Cross as a tree. In its opening lines, the object the dreamer sees is repeatedly called a *treow* (tree): 'tree of glory', 'the best of trees'. The usual Old English word for the Cross, *rod* (rood), is deliberately avoided until later in the poem. (The title *The Dream of the Rood* is an invention of modern editors and gives away what the poem is careful to conceal in this opening vision.) The language of the poem is ambiguous, enhancing the sense of a shifting, paradoxical vision. The Cross is called *beama beorhtost*, 'brightest of beams', and *beam* here bears a double meaning, as it does in modern English; it's both a shaft of light and a pillar of timber. The Cross is, somehow, both these things at the same time. But most importantly, it is a tree – and a tree that has a voice, a memory, a personality.

The idea of the Cross as a sacred tree of life is not confined to the Anglo-Saxon world; it's widespread in medieval culture, found throughout the Middle Ages

in Christian art, preaching and poetry. Modern
iconography of the Crucifixion usually depicts the
Cross as simple planks of wood, hewn into shape
and no longer looking much like a living tree.
Medieval artists, however, often emphasise the tree-
like qualities of the Cross, making it impossible to
forget that this wood once grew from the earth.
Artists show this in various ways, by depicting
the knots in the timber or colouring the Cross a
naturalistic bark-brown or a vivid bright green.
Sometimes the Cross has little twigs and tendrils
springing from it, as if the tree is still sprouting
growth. More stylised forms of iconography may
show Christ nailed to a living tree still rooted in the
earth or fixed to some other kind of vine or plant;
one late-medieval tradition presents him crucified
on a lily, the symbol of his mother Mary.

The imagery of the Cross as a tree regularly
features in medieval liturgy too. One significant
influence on *The Dream of the Rood* must have
been Latin hymns such as the sixth-century *Crux
Fidelis*, that sets the Cross in comparison with
other trees of the forest:

> Faithful Cross, among all others
> the one most noble tree;
> no wood can bear such surpassing
> foliage, blossom or fruit.
> Sweet wood, sweet nails,
> upholding so sweet a weight!

It is Christ himself who is the blossom and fruit of
this tree, its 'sweet weight'. This hymn, and others
which imagine the Cross as a living tree, would be
sung on Good Friday and on the two feasts in the
church's year dedicated specifically to the Cross,
which fall in May and September – in spring and
autumn, when trees are laden with blossom or
with fruit. On such occasions, medieval worship-
pers would see the Cross lifted up for veneration
and adorned with gold, jewels and bright drapery,
very much as the tree appears in the opening of
The Dream of the Rood. The personification of the
Cross as *fidelis*, faithful, also seems to inform the

Fragment of an Anglo-Saxon cross from around the late seventh century, one of the earliest
runic inscriptions discovered in Britain. Church of Saint Mary and Saint Michael, Great Urswick.

poem's emphasis on the Cross's steadfast loyalty, that endures despite its fear and pain: 'I trembled when that man embraced me,' it says, 'yet I dared not bow to the ground; I had to stand fast.'

This way of envisioning the Cross as a real tree, with leaves and branches, blossom and fruit, had profound consequences for medieval thinking about the Crucifixion. It underlined the parallels between the Cross and the tree in the Garden of Eden: 'through a tree came to us death, when Adam ate the forbidden fruit, and through a tree came to us again life and redemption, when Christ hung on the Cross to redeem us', as one Anglo-Saxon writer put it. The pairing of the trees connects the sin and the redemption, the sickness and the remedy – the tree of death and the tree of life.

It also offered poignant ways of thinking about Christ himself, the blossom of the tree. It's no coincidence that medieval poetry about the Crucifixion, most appropriate to read around Eastertime, is full of imagery of blossoming trees; it reflects what people would be seeing around them, the natural world bursting into life and beauty. The new life brought by Christ's death on the Cross was mirrored and recalled by the rejuvenation of springtime. 'When I see blossoms spring and hear the birds' song, my heart is stung with a sweet love-longing', begins one English poem of the 14th century. The speaker goes on to explain that this love-longing is for Christ, who himself was 'stung' by love when he was nailed to the tree. The blossoming of the trees has brought Christ's suffering to the speaker's mind, leading to a sudden, heart-piercing stab of love, sharp as a spear. Blossom and birdsong, among the most beautiful experiences the natural world has to offer, bring thoughts of suffering and death, and a love so powerful that it becomes painful. The image of Christ as a blossom might at first glance seem sentimental, but its nuances are moving, yoking together death and life, bliss and pain, natural growth and a terrible distortion of the beauty of nature. Christ on the tree has not grown like a blossom; he is hung there as a dying man.

This juxtaposition of death and new life is also evident in the iconography of Christ crucified on a lily, which is sometimes found in conjunction with images of the Annunciation. In the Middle Ages, the Annunciation and Good Friday were widely thought to have taken place on the same date, 25 March, so that Christ died on the same date he was conceived; his death and conception unite, completing the full circle of his life on earth. The Virgin is often linked with scriptural images of the tree or the vine, such as the root of Jesse, and medi-

---

Mary and the Cross are alike in having honour and life-giving power. They are also partners in grief.

---

eval liturgy on Marian feasts was rich in imagery of life-giving trees. This gives Mary a particular parallel with the tree of the Cross, another created being chosen by God to play a unique role in the salvation of mankind. The Cross in *The Dream of the Rood* compares itself to Mary, saying that God chose to honour her above all human beings, just as he honoured the tree of the Cross above all creatures of the natural world.

Their honour and their life-giving power were not all Mary and the Cross had in common; they were also partners in grief. One medieval poetic tradition imagines a dialogue between Mary and the Cross, in which both express their anguish at Christ's death. Mary begins by fiercely upbraiding the Cross for its cruelty to her child, 'my Fruit', as she calls him. He is the fruit of her body, tenderly nurtured, and she cannot bear the thought that he is now hanging exposed to the elements, left to rot like an overripe apple. In her agony of grief, she blames the Cross. But the Cross protests that

---

Opposite: Fifteenth-century glass-painting at Holy Trinity Church in Long Melford, Suffolk, showing the figure of Christ nailed to a lily.

it loves this Fruit too; it would never have chosen the role that has been given to it, but it must do as it has been commanded. In order to become the remedy for the apple of the Garden of Eden, God chose to become both the fruit of Mary's body, loved and cherished, and the fruit of the Cross, broken and torn – crushed so that the juices of life might flow.

Though a speaking tree may seem strange to our modern imaginations, *The Dream of the Rood* has much in common with Anglo-Saxon riddles, that give voices to all kinds of objects, from an inkhorn to a bucket, a plough to a ship's anchor. Like the tree in *The Dream of the Rood*, these objects have their own stories, memories and emotions. The plough describes how hard it is to work with its nose in the earth; the shield talks about the scars and wounds it has received in battle; the anchor tells how it feels to be buffeted by the waves. The stories these objects tell are often narratives of transformation: they have begun their existence in one form and then, carved or stripped or hammered into shape, have taken on a new identity as objects used in human society. Many have been constructed from organic materials – wood, leather, bone or feathers – and they seem to carry within them a memory of the living creatures they came from, even after they have been pressed into service by human beings. In one riddle, a leather shoe remembers that it used to be part of an ox, a powerful creature killed so that its skin could be literally trodden into the earth. In another, an inkhorn, made from the antler of a stag, wistfully recalls its journeys on the stag's lofty head, before it was captured and forcibly repurposed for human use. Very often these transformations are imagined as violent, unwanted and painful; the inkhorn's account of having its insides carved out to hold ink is particularly gruesome. In parting from the animals who bore them, these objects have undergone a kind of death, yet through their difficult

transformations they are given a new life in the human world.

In *The Dream of the Rood*, the Cross too experiences a process of violent transformation. Ripped from its root and forced to share in Christ's agony, it undergoes suffering as painful as any in the riddles. Once again the inflictors of this violence are human beings, blindly causing pain to serve their own ends; the men who cut down the tree have no idea what they're doing to it, any more than we think about how our shoes feel when we walk on them. Through its transformative suffering, though, the Cross too acquires a new identity – no longer an ordinary tree but the tree of life, connecting heaven and earth. At a key moment, as Christ is nailed to the Cross, it announces its new and glorious purpose: 'As a rood I was raised up; I lifted the mighty King'.

This tree, stained with blood and adorned with jewels, is a meeting-point of extremes, a place of paradox. It is simultaneously a symbol of horror and beauty, shame and glory, suffering and joy. But really, of course, all this is not about the suffering of the Cross; that is merely a poetic conceit, like the riddles of the inkhorn and the leather shoe. The suffering is Christ's. Though *The Dream of the Rood* offers an unforgettable alternative perspective on the events of the Crucifixion, it's not so much about the Cross itself as it is an attempt to help its audience approach the central strangeness of the Christian story: the idea that an all-powerful God should choose to place himself in the hands of human enemies, willingly undergo suffering, to take on himself the punishment for mankind's many sins. The tree didn't choose to suffer, to become the Cross, any more than the antler chose to be turned into an inkhorn or than any human being can choose the forms of suffering that come to us and transform us. But God chose to suffer. Through that suffering, the poem suggests, it is not he but we who are transformed, given life and made into something new. ⤳

The Way of the Passion

Andreas Felger, *The Five Wounds of Christ*,
oil on canvas

Five readings from across the centuries illuminate the meaning of suffering in Christian discipleship.

Felicity of Carthage

✦

Anselm of Canterbury

✦

Julian of Norwich

✦

Martin Luther

✦

J Heinrich Arnold

Andreas Felger, *Credo VI: Suffered under Pontius Pilate*,
oil on canvas, 2011

Felicity of Carthage

*This third-century eyewitness account describes the martyrdom
of Felicity, an enslaved woman, and her companions.*

Felicity, who had been with child when she was arrested, was sorrowful as the day of the games drew near, fearing lest for this cause she should be kept back (for it is not lawful for women that are with child to be brought forth for torment) and lest she should shed her holy and innocent blood after the rest, among strangers and malefactors. Also her fellow martyrs were much afflicted lest they should leave behind them so good a friend. Wherefore with united groaning they poured out their prayer to the Lord, three days before the games. Immediately after their prayer her pains came upon her. And when because of the natural difficulty of the eighth month she was oppressed with her travail and made complaint, one of the servants said to her: 'You who complain now, what will you do when you are thrown to the beasts, which you scorned when you would not sacrifice?' She answered, 'I now suffer what I suffer myself, but there another shall be within me who will suffer for me, because I am to suffer for him.' So she was delivered of a daughter, whom a sister brought up as her own.

Now dawned the day of their victory and they went forth from the prison into the amphitheatre as it were into heaven, cheerful and bright of countenance; if they trembled at all, it was for joy, not for fear. Felicity, rejoicing that she had borne a child in safety, that she might fight with the beasts, came now from blood to blood, from the midwife to the gladiator, to wash after her travail in a second baptism.

Adapted from *The Passion of Perpetua and Felicity*, trans W H Shewring (1931).

Andreas Felger, *Credo VII: Crucified*,
oil on canvas, 2011

Anselm of Canterbury

*Saint Anselm (ca 1033–1109) was a Benedictine monk,
Christian philosopher and scholar.*

My Lord and my Creator,
you bear with me and nourish me—
be my helper.
I thirst for you, I hunger for you, I desire you,
I sigh for you, I covet you:
I am like an orphan deprived of the presence
of a very kind father,
who, weeping and wailing,
does not cease to cling to the dear face
with his whole heart.
So, as much as I can,
though not as much as I ought,
I am mindful of your passion,
your buffeting, your scourging, your cross,
your wounds,
how you were slain for me,
how prepared for burial and buried;
and also I remember your glorious Resurrection,
and wonderful Ascension.
All this I hold with unwavering faith,
and weep over the hardship of exile,
hoping in the sole consolation of your coming,
ardently longing for the glorious contemplation
of your face.

Saint Anselm, 'Prayer to Christ', from *Second Letter to the
Countess Mathilda*, trans Benedicta Ward.

Andreas Felger, *Credo VIII: And Buried,*
oil on canvas, 2011

Julian of Norwich

*The 14th-century anchorite recounts receiving a vision in
which Jesus explains to her why he suffered the Passion.*

Then said our good Lord Jesus Christ: *Art thou well pleased that I suffered for thee?* I said: *Yea, good Lord, I thank Thee; Yea, good Lord, blessed mayst Thou be.* Then said Jesus, our kind Lord: *If thou art pleased, I am pleased: it is a joy, a bliss, an endless satisfying to me that ever suffered I Passion for thee; and if I might suffer more, I would suffer more...*

And in these words: *If that I might suffer more, I would suffer more* – I saw in truth that as often as He might die, so often He would, and love should never let Him have rest till He had done it. And I beheld with great diligence for to learn how often He would die if He might. And verily the number passed mine understanding and my wits so far that my reason might not, nor could, comprehend it. And when He had thus oft died, or should, yet He would set it at nought, for love: for all seemeth Him but little in regard of His love...

Beholding in this blessed Passion *the love that made Him to suffer passeth as far all His pains as Heaven is above Earth.* For the pains was a noble, worshipful deed done in a time by the working of love: but Love was without beginning, is and shall be without ending. For which love He said full sweetly these words: *If I might suffer more, I would suffer more.* He said not, If it were needful to suffer more: for though it were not needful, if He might suffer more, He would.

Julian of Norwich, *Revelations of Divine Love,* trans Grace Warrack (Methuen & Company, 1901), 47–49.

Andreas Felger, *Credo IX: Descended into the Realm of Death*,
oil on canvas, 2011

Martin Luther

*The great 16th-century Reformer imagines Christ speaking to
a disciple about what it means to follow him.*

Discipleship is not limited to what you can comprehend – it must transcend all comprehension. Plunge into the deep waters beyond your own comprehension, and I will help you to comprehend even as I do. Bewilderment is the true comprehension. Not to know where you are going is the true knowledge. My comprehension transcends yours.

Thus Abraham went forth from his father, and not knowing whither he went. He trusted himself to my knowledge and cared not for his own, and thus he took the right road and came to his journey's end. Behold, that is the way of the cross. You cannot find it in yourself, so you must let me lead you as though you were a blind man. Wherefore, it is not you, no man, no living creature, but I myself who instruct you by my word and Spirit in the way you should go. Not the work which you choose, not the suffering you devise, but the road which is clean contrary to all that you choose or contrive or desire – that is the road you must take. To that I call you and in that you must be my disciple. If you do that, there is the acceptable time, and there your master is come.

Martin Luther, as quoted in Dietrich Bonhoeffer, *The Cost of Discipleship* (Touchstone, 1995), 93.

Andreas Felger, *Credo XI: Ascended into Heaven*,
oil on canvas, 2011

J Heinrich Arnold

In his classic work on discipleship, the Bruderhof pastor
(1913–1982) describes the via amara, *'the bitter way'.*

Dying with Christ does not mean being extinguished. But it does mean pouring out our innermost being before him, bringing our sins to the cross and becoming one with him who died for us.

When a grain of wheat is laid in the earth, it dies. It no longer remains a grain, but through death it brings forth fruit. This is the way of true Christianity. It is the way Jesus went when he died on the cross for each of us. If we want our lives to be fruits of Christ's death on the cross, we cannot remain individual grains. We must be ready to die too.

Have Christ before you in everything so that you are able to die for him! Long to come nearer to him. Live in one spirit – in service to him – so that the grace of God may always be with you. Then, even when the day comes that your blood must be shed for him, you will be joyful. It will be nothing but victory!

Jesus says that if we love him and fulfil his commandments, he will love us and disclose himself to us. This is not a question of a theology or a teaching but a question of life, of receiving Jesus as a real person, as the Son of Man who wants to love us and reveal himself to us. When we dwell in Jesus, he will dwell in us and we can say like Paul the Apostle, 'I live, yet not I, but Christ liveth in me.'

J Heinrich Arnold, *Discipleship* (Plough, 1994), 247.

God's Purpose in Your Pain

What good could suffering possibly serve?

RICK WARREN

Bᴇᴄᴀᴜsᴇ ᴡᴇ ʟɪᴠᴇ in a world broken by sin, life is painful. Almost everyone is living with some kind of pain. The type varies – it may be physical, relational, mental, emotional, financial, social or spiritual – but it all hurts. Pain is inevitable; none of us is able to opt out of it.

As a minister for 50 years, I've spent my life helping people in pain and I've never had to look far to find it. To cope with this reality, we desensitise ourselves and detach ourselves from others who are suffering. One of the great challenges in my ministry has been to stay sensitive while witnessing so much distress.

One way God has kept me empathetic towards others' pain has been by giving me what the apostle Paul calls 'a thorn in the flesh' (2 Cor 12:7). I've lived with chronic pain for most of my adult life. As I was writing this article, I had to pause for my fifth hospitalisation in a year. So what I'm sharing with you is not just theory, but truths learned through pain that have enabled me to carry on in spite of it. I've learned that pain should not be wasted, but used for God's purposes.

Scripture is clear that following Christ doesn't exempt us from suffering. Instead we're told to expect it (1 Pet 4:12, John 16:33) and to consider suffering for Christ a privilege (Phil 1:29). Peter says, 'Those who suffer according to God's will should commit themselves to their faithful Creator and continue to do good' (1 Pet 4:19). Submitting to God's will does not protect you from suffering. In fact, sometimes doing the right thing creates pain.

Both believers and unbelievers experience trials. But Christians have a hope to hold on to that not only comforts us, but also empowers us to bless others.

What is our hope in pain? It is the promise of God that he can bring good out of anything, even pain, if we trust him. Romans 8:28 is one of the most beloved verses in the Bible, but it's also one of the most misquoted. It does not say, 'All things that happen to us are good.' That is obviously untrue: rape, cancer, war, disease, racism and starvation are not good. It also does not say, 'All things will have a happy ending.' That too is not reality: not every injustice is corrected; not every disease is healed; not every pain is removed. Here is what the apostle Paul actually says:

'And we *know*...' We don't have to guess or wonder or doubt. We can be certain.

'That in *all* things...' This includes our hurts, mistakes, sins, genetics and experiences, and even what others do to us.

'God *works* for the good...' Not everything is good, but God is always working for our good in everything. Anyone can bring good out of good,

but God can bring good out of evil. He turns crucifixions into resurrections.

'Of those who love him...' This is not a blanket promise to everyone experiencing pain. If I'm living in rebellion against my Creator's plan for me or if I reject God's love, everything will work towards my destruction and death (Prov 16:18, 25).

'Who have been called according to his *purpose*'. The key to our hope is understanding God's purpose for our lives, including our pain. Only then will we find meaning, benefit and even joy in our suffering.

SCRIPTURE POINTS to five purposes God has for his children while we're here on earth:

I We are here to learn to *know and love Christ*. God made you so he could love you, and he wants you to love him back. Expressing our love to God is called worship.

II We are here to learn to *love Christ's family*. God formed you for his family. Repeatedly, the Bible tells us that it is impossible to love God and not love his family. We are called to belong, not just believe. This is called fellowship.

III We are here to learn to *grow in Christ*. You were created to become like Christ. God wants you to grow to spiritual maturity, and our model is Jesus himself. This is called discipleship.

IV We are here to learn to *serve Christ*. God did not create you to serve yourself but to serve him, and here on earth we serve him by serving others in Jesus's name. Jesus says, 'Only those who throw away their lives for my sake...will ever know what it means to really live' (Mark 8:35). This is called ministry.

V We are here to learn to *share Christ*. Once we've accepted the good news, God expects us to pass it on to others. This is called evangelism.

Rick Warren is the founding pastor of Saddleback Church, teacher for the Daily Hope Broadcast and chairman of the Finishing the Task coalition.

Vinicius Barajas, *Easter Triptych I*, 2018

God establishes and develops these purposes in our lives through the Word of God renewing our minds (John 17:17), through the Spirit of God transforming our character (2 Cor 3:17–18) and through the often painful circumstances of life causing us to make choices (James 1:2–4).

I

Worship

Anytime something painful happens in your life, you have a choice. You can run *to* God or you can run *from* God. As a pastor, I've been involved in relief efforts after natural disasters in many countries. From those experiences I've noticed that in a crisis, typically about half the people run *towards* God with their pain and about half run *away* from God. That makes no sense to me. Why would I run from the only one who fully understands all the emotions I'm feeling? And why would I avoid the only one able to heal and restore me?

Our most passionate prayers are when we are in the most pain. No one prays perfunctory prayers when they're in pain. Superficial prayers are replaced by genuine cries of the heart.

Ten years ago, my youngest son, who had struggled since childhood with mental illness, took his life in a moment of deep depression. It was the worst day of my life. My wife, Kay, and I and our other children were devastated. I've never felt such suffocating and paralysing pain. What saved my sanity in the following months was spending hours, and even days, alone with God in worship, pouring out all my jumbled emotions. I used my pain to draw closer to God.

What I learned was that we draw closer to God by telling him exactly how we feel, not by telling him what we think he wants us to feel. God wants the real, not the ideal, from you. In pain, you cry out. You argue with God. You complain to God. You express all the negative emotions you're feeling. You don't suppress them, you confess them.

Complaining to God when you're in pain is a biblical act of worship – it's called lamenting. One-third of the 150 psalms in the Book of Psalms are psalms of lament. I learned to lament by praying those 50 psalms. Worship is not always celebration, praise and thanksgiving. Expressing every aspect of grief – shock, sorrow, struggle, surrender – can bring you closer to God too.

All your emotions are God-given. You have emotions because you're made in God's image, and God is an emotional God. In the Bible, God feels and expresses anger, grief, jealousy, frustration and other negative emotions that we often try to suppress.

The apostle Paul used his suffering to draw closer to God: 'We were under great pressure, far beyond our ability to endure, so that we despaired even of life itself. Indeed, we felt we had received the sentence of death. But this happened that we might not rely on ourselves but on God, who raises the dead' (2 Cor 1:8–9). Later, Paul writes to the Corinthians about the effect of their sorrow as a result of the letter he had sent them: 'I'm glad I sent it, not because it hurt you but because the pain turned you to God' (2 Cor 7:9).

II
Fellowship

We typically think we will attract others by impressing them with our successes, victories and accomplishments. But talking about those things can create jealousy, competition and distance between people. In contrast, sharing our weaknesses, failures and grief creates a common bond.

Pain is the great equaliser because it is indiscriminate. Pain pays no attention to status, wealth, religion, education, age or gender. Loss is a universal common denominator. So if you want to draw others closer to you in fellowship, dare to be vulnerable. That requires being honest with God and yourself first. It requires allowing others to see you in your pain and to bear your burden.

The day our youngest child lost his battle with mental illness and ended his life, Kay and I stood on the driveway of his home hugging and sobbing while awaiting the police. Within about 20 minutes of hearing the news, our small-group fellowship from our church showed up. On that driveway, the men gathered around me and held me tightly in a group hug while the women did the same with Kay. They didn't say much, because no words were adequate for the agony we felt. They just hugged us. Finally one said, 'There's nothing we can say, but we're not leaving you alone tonight.' They drove us home and they all slept on the floor and in chairs in our living room and kitchen. It was the ministry of presence: show up and shut up.

People who have little pain in their lives can be unsympathetic, even judgemental, towards those for whom life is a constant, painful struggle. On the other hand, if you choose to allow it to, personal pain will increase your sensitivity to others' pain, deepen your empathy for their suffering and enable you to connect with people you otherwise have little in common with.

Vinicius Barajas, *Easter Triptych II*, 2018

III

Discipleship

God's goal is for us to become more like Christ. That leads to two questions. First, what is Jesus really like? Galatians says, 'The fruit of the Spirit is love, joy, peace, forbearance, kindness, goodness, faithfulness, gentleness and self-control' (Gal 5:22–23). That's a portrait of Jesus and to become Christlike is to have these qualities in our lives.

That leads to the second question: *How* does God make us more like Jesus? The answer is by taking us through experiences like those Jesus went through. Were there times when Jesus was lonely? Frustrated? Misunderstood? Criticised? Were there times when he experienced pain? Hebrews says, 'Even though Jesus was God's son, he learned obedience from the things he suffered' (Heb 5:8).

We learn obedience the same way – through painful situations. Hebrews continues, 'Suffering made Jesus perfect' (Heb 5:9). If God used suffering to develop Jesus, we should expect him to use the same on us.

There is no situation we cannot grow from if we choose to respond correctly. Every problem or pressure is an opportunity to grow in Christlikeness. We can even grow from temptation, because temptation is just a choice between what's right and what's wrong. Every time we choose what's right when tempted, we grow more like Christ.

How does God produce the fruit of the Spirit in our lives? By putting us in the exact opposite circumstance. We learn to love when God puts hard-to-love people around us. We learn joy in the midst of grief. We learn inner peace in the midst of chaos. We learn patience by being forced to wait. Every point of pain will either become a stepping stone to maturity or a stumbling block that keeps us stuck in immaturity.

There are some lessons we learn only through pain. The paraphrase of 2 Corinthians 7:11 in *The Message* version mentions nine possible benefits: 'Isn't it wonderful all the ways in which this distress has goaded you closer to God? You're more alive, more concerned, more sensitive, more reverent, more human, more passionate, more responsible. Looked at from any angle, you've come out of this with purity of heart.'

IV
Ministry

Paul speaks of pain in connection with ministry in 2 Corinthians:

> [God] comforts us in all our troubles so that we can comfort others. When they are troubled, we will be able to give them the same comfort God has given us. For the more we suffer for Christ, the more God will shower us with his comfort through Christ. Even when we are weighed down with troubles, it is for your comfort and salvation! For when we ourselves are comforted, we will certainly comfort you. Then you can patiently endure the same things we suffer. (2 Cor 1:4–6)

Notice the phrase 'when we are weighed down with troubles, it is *for your comfort*'. Just as God in Christ suffered for our benefit, sometimes God allows us to experience pain in order that we might use it to minister to others who are in pain.

Of course, God uses our strengths and talents to help others, but often in even more powerful and transforming ways, God uses our weaknesses and failures. Paul explains this in 2 Corinthians: 'If I must boast, I will boast of the things that show my weakness…[The Lord] said to me, "My grace is sufficient for you, for my power is made perfect in weakness."…That is why, for Christ's sake, I delight in weaknesses…for when I am weak, then I am strong' (2 Cor 11:30; 12:9–10).

Who could better empathise with someone going through a divorce than those who have experienced it themselves? Who could better minister to someone with an addiction or a chronic illness or depression than someone who has struggled with the same issue?

Every painful experience you've gone through in your life is a ministry opportunity. You can use both the pain you've already gone through *and* the pain that you are currently going through to help others who are experiencing the same painful circumstances.

You might be thinking, 'But I have never found a solution or cure!' That should not stop you. We all face losses and pains that may never be cured or resolved on this side of heaven. Not every prayer for healing is answered the way we want. Life is filled with unsolvable problems, terminal diseases, lifelong disabilities and chronic pain that will have to wait for the ultimate cure in eternity. Still, people need encouragement and support and they need to be taught how to *manage* what cannot be changed.

Or you might be thinking, 'But I'm still struggling with this myself.' That makes you even more relatable, because you're dealing with it on a daily basis. God wants to use your pain *now*, while you're in the messy middle of it, when you haven't figured out all the answers. If God used only perfect people, nothing would ever get done. Everything good and helpful that has ever been accomplished on earth was done by imperfect people, doing it imperfectly.

Your suffering may be disappointment, like wanting to be married but being unable to find a spouse or wanting to have children but being

Vinicius Barajas, *Easter Triptych III*, 2018

unable to. What do you do then, when the way seems blocked? You *redirect* your love. There are plenty of lonely people in the world who need your love. And there are plenty of children who need to be cared for. Instead of focusing on what you've lost or never had, redirect your focus to helping others.

Jesus wants to redeem your suffering. What does that mean? Redemptive suffering uses your pain to help other people. Raising a child who struggled with mental illness, Kay and I both knew that our calling would include ministering to others in similar situations. And when we had to face our son's suicide, we knew that helping other families devastated by suicide would become part of our calling too. It is not a ministry that we aspired to, but almost every week, God brings people into our lives who need help dealing with either mental illness or suicide. We're not wasting our pain.

V

Evangelism

Our pain may be the most powerful tool for bringing others to Christ and fulfilling his 'Great Commission' to make disciples of all people. It may also be the least utilised tool. I have 500 books on evangelism in my library, yet I don't remember reading anything about using pain as our greatest witness.

There are a number of reasons I believe sharing

our pain is the most powerful evangelistic approach. First, Jesus did not remain aloof from our pain. He bore our sins and entered into our suffering and pain, all the way to the point of death, and his suffering and death and resurrection are good news that gives hope to the suffering today. Second, pain is universal. It is the great equaliser of humanity, the common denominator through all cultures and ages. Everybody is hurting somehow, so sharing how we hurt is a natural bridge-builder to literally anyone! Third,

---

> **The greatest witness of God's love in all of history was not Jesus's perfect life. It was not his teaching. It was not his miracles. The greatest witness of God's love was Christ's suffering on the cross.**

---

sharing what is hurting us adds credibility to our witness. A faith that is being tested daily by real-life troubles is worth checking out. Fourth, showing humility is endearing: we naturally like people who admit they don't have it all together instead of pretending they do.

Many Christians believe God expects us to pretend to live a perfect life in front of our non-believing neighbours. Hide our problems. Mask our pain. Cover up our sins. The result is that Christians are labelled hypocrites and phonies. Everyone already knows we don't have it all together.

What if instead we did the exact opposite? What if we Christians were vulnerable, upfront and honest about our mistakes, problems and fears?

That would be refreshing, authentic and attractive. Unbelievers have the same problems we do. They can't see how we deal with our problems biblically if we're always hiding them. In many ways, Christians have it all wrong. We think people are impressed by our *prosperity*. But actually, they're more impressed with how we handle *adversity*. It's not our success but how we handle suffering that gives our witness credibility.

The apostle Paul knew this well. Writing to the church in Philippi about all the pain he'd experienced as a prisoner in Rome, he says, 'I want you to know, my dear brothers and sisters, that everything that has happened to me here has helped to spread the Good News' (Phil 1:12). And in a letter to the church in Corinth, he says, 'In everything we do, we show that we are true ministers of God. We patiently endure troubles and hardships and calamities of every kind' (2 Cor 6:4). Just as your greatest ministry is likely to arise out of your deepest pain, your greatest witness to unbelievers is likely to arise out of how you handle it.

Many Christians think they only have one testimony: the story of how they came to faith in Christ. But your experience of pain is a potential testimony you can share. If you've ever lost a job, a home, a loved one or a reputation and God helped you through, that's a testimony.

The greatest witness of God's love in all of history was not Jesus's perfect life. It was not his teaching. It was not his miracles. The greatest witness of God's love was Christ's suffering on the cross.

None of us can control what happens to us in life. But we do get to choose our response. We can choose whether we will waste our pain or learn from it and use it to help others. Instead of asking yourself, 'Why is this happening to me?' start asking God two other questions: 'What do you want me to learn?' and 'Whom do you want me to help?'

Editors' Picks

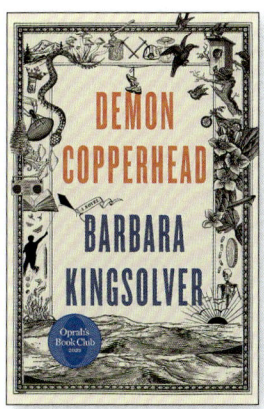

Demon Copperhead
A Novel

*By Barbara Kingsolver
(Harper, 560 pages)*

Franz Kafka once wrote, 'If what we are reading does not wake us, as with a fist hammering on our skulls, then why do we read it? Good God, what we need…are books that hit us like an axe to break the frozen sea within us.' Barbara Kingsolver's *Demon Copperhead* is such a book. Not for the fainthearted, it seethes with the raw energy of its foul-mouthed teen protagonist as it follows him through a childhood marked by domestic violence, addiction and loss. The denouement contains glimmers of rehabilitation, but it's the elusiveness of tidy resolutions that keeps the novel moving.

Charles Dickens's *David Copperfield*, which inspired this novel, follows the trials of a young Englishman whose grit helps him navigate life in 19th-century London's underbelly; Kingsolver's reimagining is set in the 1990s in a vastly different but equally bleak milieu: her native Appalachia.

Readers seeking the idealised beauty of rural Americana will not find it here. True, trilliums brighten the hollows in spring and there are breathtaking mountaintop views. But forget Robert Frost: this landscape is scarred by defunct coal mines and failing farms, littered with dollar stores and pain clinics. Socially, too, there is wreckage – 'trailer trash' and truck-stop whores, unscrupulous doctors who demand sexual favours for prescriptions, burned-out social workers and fraudulent strivers. Not a family seems immune to the ravages of the opioid epidemic; everyone knows someone in prison or foster care or someone who has OD'd.

Kingsolver's Appalachia is as much a state of mind as a region; like the hills that hem it in, the malaise has trapped generations. Even those who follow the lures of the world beyond never truly escape but often return, jaded by empty promises of advancement or fleeing the jaws of big-city life.

If this were reality TV, you might switch channels. But it's not. Nor is it poverty porn – there's nothing gratuitous. Indeed, Kingsolver's novel rings with the authenticity of autobiography. As she has noted, her parents seemed to be leaning over her as she wrote, speaking to her 'in a language that my years outside Appalachia tried to shame from my tongue'. Perhaps that's why, instead of appearing as stock figures, her characters leap from the page as vibrant individuals so real that you might be tempted to Google them.

And if, as at least one reviewer has charged, they seem to lack agency, that's just the point the author appears to be making. Stuck in a whirlpool of institutional poverty, most of them (like the actual people who inspired them) have little hope of ever getting out. In bringing their travails to the page, Kingsolver confronts us with that reality. To quote the dedication embedded in her acknowledgements, 'For the kids who wake up hungry in dark places every day, who've lost their families to poverty and pain pills…who feel invisible or wish they were: this book is for you.'

—*Chris Zimmerman,
a member of the Bruderhof*

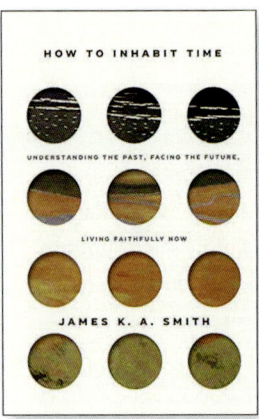

How to Inhabit Time
Understanding the Past, Facing the Future, Living Faithfully Now

*By James K A Smith
(Brazos Press, 208 pages)*

How to Inhabit Time is a curious book, braiding in many strands of concern and style: personal memoir, philosophical reflection and devotional meditation. Its central fascination is how we as human beings are formed by being creatures who live in time, how our histories, personal and generational, shape the way we live, worship and heal. Smith writes, 'A rolling stone might carry no moss, but a temporal human being picks up and carries an entire history as they roll through a lifetime'. A substantial portion of the book features Smith's reckoning with his own history, recollecting a long season of depression springing from his buried grief over his father's abandonment and the healing grace of therapy that helped him live with this broken history. These sections display a new energy and craft in Smith's writing, distinct from his prior work. I found myself eager for more of this mode, wishing Smith would give it full rein.

Smith has other concerns to attend to, however. He also wants to explore time's philosophical dimensions and to consider how temporality frames the very conditions of our existence and perception. He draws largely on the phenomenology of Edmund Husserl and Martin Heidegger, with portions of the book devoted to Augustine, which might feel familiar to readers of his other work. Smith explores the concept of 'thrownness' (Heidegger), horizons (Husserl) and distension (Augustine). For the most part, Smith integrates these concepts naturally and smoothly, less like an entry in the *Stanford Encyclopedia of Philosophy* and more like a gardener seeking the right tool to unearth a deep and troublesome root. Only occasionally did the piles of references to other authors become onerous to this reader.

While the core (and most compelling parts) of the book waft between memoir and philosophical *pensées*, Smith also devotes a significant portion of the book to his concerns for the church and particularly the American church, which he thinks lives in 'Nowhen' (a play on the idea of nowhere). Smith warns that those who 'imagine themselves wholly governed by timeless principles, unchanging convictions, expressing an idealism that assumes they are wholly governed by eternal ideas untainted by history…are oblivious to the deposits of history in their own unconscious. They have never considered the archaeological strata in their own souls'. In particular, he addresses the wound of racial injustice in America, warning that if churches continue to forget their historic failure in this area, the wound will continue to fester. This strong call for reckoning is nourished by the devotional structure of the book, that invites readers to reflect on various passages in Ecclesiastes, to reckon with their own histories and to place them into God's hands.

The result is an interesting, sometimes moving, often compelling book. If occasionally it meanders, drags or races, that is merely a reminder that so too does our experience of time and indeed, life itself.

*—Joy Clarkson,
Books and Culture Editor at* Plough

Faith, Hope and Carnage

By Nick Cave and Seán O'Hagan (Farrar, Straus and Giroux, 304 pages)

It's hard to overstate what a cult figure Nick Cave is, adored both by long-time fans of his rock band, Nick Cave and the Bad Seeds and by more recent disciples of his online advice column, The Red Hand Files. Famously a former heroin addict with an abrasive stage persona, Cave is instantly recognisable: a modern vampire in a slick suit and long black hair. But in 2015, Cave lost his 15-year-old son Arthur in a tragic cliff fall. The loss has brought a new softness, a man grieving in public, making meaning (and art) from the unbearable, and doing it with an unusual level of honesty and humanity.

It is this humanity to which *Faith, Hope and Carnage* attests. This record of conversations between Seán O'Hagan (an arts and culture writer) and Cave explores grief, creativity and a whole lot of religion, that Cave calls 'spirituality with rigour'. O'Hagan, raised Catholic during Northern Ireland's Troubles, distrusts the church, while Cave is increasingly drawn to it. The combination of these perspectives is electric.

Those without an interest in religion will still find much in the book, but what I found so radically refreshing is the unabashed longing for God. What becomes clear is that this longing is not a new theme for Cave, even though long-time fans like O'Hagan failed to see how serious Cave was in his search. Biblical imagery is everywhere in Cave's albums, but the goth styling leads listeners to assume these references are more profane than sacred. On the contrary, we learn that in the years of Cave's addiction, he was 'in and out of church'. However, while lots of people were happy to take drugs with Cave, no one would go with him to a church service. Echoing Jung's '*spiritus contra spiritum*' – the spiritual as a remedy for addiction – Cave tells O'Hagan, 'Using heroin and the need for a sacred dimension to life were similar pursuits, in that they were attempts, at that time, to remedy the same condition.' *Which was?* 'A kind of emptiness, I guess, and a hunger.' *A hunger for what?* 'More.'

Bereavement has led Cave to speak more openly about God, church and his desire for more. While

'I think I would be happier if I stopped window shopping and just stepped through the door.'
—Nick Cave

the more familiar story is that grief causes crises of faith, for Cave 'in this dark place, the idea of God feels more present or maybe more essential. It actually feels like grief and God are somehow intertwined.' I couldn't help sketching a cross in the margin.

O'Hagan's respectful scepticism and Cave's 'increasing impatience' with his own non-committal religious explorations lead to a circling around doubt and hope and longing that reads like a conversation held late at night, over a bottle of wine with someone you trust not to laugh at you. To witness a friendship of this vulnerability, especially between two later-life, hard-bitten music men is deeply moving. O'Hagan is clearly worried a full-blown conversion would be bad for Cave's art, but doesn't argue when Cave says wistfully, 'I think I would be happier if I stopped window shopping and just stepped through the door.'

—Elizabeth Oldfield,
podcast host, The Sacred

The Water and the Blood

To find home, we must first lose it.

JULIAN WALDNER

'IT BEGAN IN SWITZERLAND,' wrote Kaspar Braitmichel, the 16th-century Hutterite chronicler, 'where God brought about an awakening'. The year was 1525. In Zurich a group of young men led by the city's reforming pastor, Ulrich Zwingli, had been gathering to discuss matters of theology and the new humanistic learning. Two of them, Felix Manz and Conrad Grebel, had worked alongside Zwingli to bring about changes in the city's churches and institutions on the basis of their study of the New Testament. Their initial proposals – abolishing mandatory fast days, conducting church services in the vernacular instead of Latin and cracking down on the lucrative custom of hiring out local sons as mercenaries – had been supported by the city council, giving Zwingli growing political influence.

Julian Waldner is a member of the Decker Hutterite Community in southwestern Manitoba, Canada, and a first-year student at Canadian Mennonite University.

But Manz, Grebel and their supporters had come to believe that, according to scripture, the act of becoming a Christian must be voluntary, not a civic duty enforced by state coercion. Accordingly, baptism should occur only when an individual is mature enough to freely confess his or her faith and commit to Christian discipleship. Zwingli, despite at first sympathising with his friends' argument, balked at actually abandoning infant baptism. After all, attacking this time-honoured practice struck at the foundation of a society in which church and state were closely intertwined. To press for such a radical rupture, Zwingli believed, would endanger the reform cause in Zurich and beyond. A public debate culminated in the city council issuing an ultimatum: the dissenters had eight days to baptise their infants; if they continued to refuse, they would be banished from the city.

Four days later, on 21 January, the radicals took a bold next step: instead of baptising their infants, they deemed their own long-ago baptisms invalid. As they were meeting that evening in Manz's house, Braitmichel records, 'fear came over them and struck their hearts'. They knelt in prayer and when they rose, Georg Blaurock requested Christian baptism from Grebel and then baptised the others. Thus the Anabaptist (their adversaries' description of 'one who baptises again') stream of the Reformation was brought into being. Anabaptism spread rapidly through the region as the dissenters preached and baptised in defiance of the authorities.

The response was swift and brutal. After two years on the run, Felix Manz was captured and drowned in the Limmat River by city authorities – the first of many Anabaptist martyrs. Blaurock was beaten and exiled the same day. (Grebel had meanwhile died of the plague while travelling as an underground evangelist.)

Yet within a few years, the Anabaptist movement they had sparked would count thousands of adherents. They faced a vicious campaign of persecution throughout the Holy Roman Empire, with around 3,000 executions and countless stories of forced migration, dispossession and family separation. Yet the movement continued to grow. Since then, some of its once-fringe insights – freedom of conscience, economic sharing and community, non-violent resistance to injustice – have become widely influential in broader society. As a Christian tradition, too, it lives on in Mennonite, Amish, Hutterite, Bruderhof and other Anabaptist churches around the globe.

I WAS BORN AND RAISED at the Decker Hutterite Community on the prairies of Manitoba, Canada. Beyond the gravel ring road that encircles our community is a vast expanse of wheat fields framed by open blue sky. It's a landscape very different from the towering Alps my ancestors beheld. Separated by thousands of miles and almost half a millennium from that first fateful baptism, my community is nonetheless a flowering of the seeds planted on that January evening.

My roots go deep into Hutterite soil, but it was only with my own baptism last Easter that I became part of what those first Anabaptists began in Zurich. The striking difference between those baptisms and mine is that while the former represented a rupture with the established tradition, my own represents a grafting onto a tradition that precedes me. Like the church that Manz and Grebel rejected through their baptism, the Hutterite church I joined is often frustratingly resistant to change and in need of reform. What does it mean to be part of a tradition that is founded on the call to break with tradition?

THE HUTTERITES EMERGED as a distinctive movement in the years after Manz, Grebel and Blaurock died. In 1528, the castle of Leonhard von Liechtenstein, an Anabaptist sympathiser in Moravia, was under threat of invasion. A group of Anabaptists pledged to support Liechtenstein in his defence of the castle, but another group – committed pacifists – would neither participate in the fighting nor accept Liechtenstein's armed protection.

Ordered to leave the castle grounds, a group of over 200 people set out. Destitute and homeless, with many orphans and widows among them, they took a defining next step: a cloak was spread on the ground where 'each one laid his possessions on it with a willing heart – without being forced – so that the needy might be supported'. From then on, they practised full community of goods, and what would later be called the Hutterite movement was born.

'We now find ourselves out in the wilderness, on a desolate heath under the open sky', wrote Jakob Hutter. 'We know of no place to go.' Hutter served as the movement's first bishop from 1533 until his death at the stake in 1536. 'In every direction we would walk straight into the jaws of robbers and tyrants, like sheep cast among ravenous wolves', he declared in this appeal to the local governor in 1535:

> We do not want to hurt or wrong anyone, not even our worst enemy...Rather than knowingly wrong a man to the value of a penny, we would let ourselves be robbed of a hundred gulden. Rather than strike our worst enemy with our hand – to say nothing of spears, swords and halberds such as the world uses – we would let our own lives be taken...You cannot simply deny us a place on the earth or in this country. The earth is the Lord's,
> and all that is in it belongs to our God in heaven.

In the years after Hutter's death, the Hutterites in Moravia were gradually able to establish thriving communities, which spread throughout the region. Newcomers were attracted from across central Europe, swelling the Hutterite population to as high as 20,000 by the end of the sixteenth century. But this relative peace came to an end with the Thirty Years' War. Plundered and brutalised by armies from all sides during the war and expelled in 1622 from Moravia, they fled across the border to Slovakia. Those Hutterites who survived into the 18th century were targeted for coerced conversion to Catholicism. A remnant fled to Transylvania, then to Wallachia and finally to Ukraine, from where their descendants (my ancestors) emigrated to North America in the 1870s.

THIS IS THE STORY I have been given – the strange story of a new thing that the God of Abraham, Isaac and Jacob began in Switzerland. Even so, my forerunners would have insisted that they were not beginning a new story but were following the same call that others had heard before them. It is a story that I did not choose for myself, and if left to my own devices it is probably not one I would choose. Yet it is my – our – story.

As a boy, I heard about the capture of the 150 men at Falkenstein and their subsequent escape, about Dirk Willems turning back to rescue his pursuer who had fallen through the ice, about the 16-year-old miller's boy who would rather go to his death than recant his faith. My grandfather vividly described his visit to the prison at Schloss Taufers, where conditions had been so humid that Hans Kräl's clothes rotted off, leaving nothing but his shirt collar.

In school we studied the history of the Reformation and the movements that preceded it, movements within the established church, such as the Cluniacs and Franciscans, as well as movements outside, such as the Albigensians, Waldensians and Hussites. We learned both to appreciate and criticise our own tradition and see the Anabaptist movement within the larger context of church history.

In the traditional sermons read at evening *Gebet* and Sunday morning *Lehr* services, the voices of our forerunners continue to speak – sometimes rather too loudly. In the songs opening each service – some written by Hutterite martyrs – the voices of our ancestors ring out from the mouths of the congregation.

Our dialect retells our story through words, vowel sounds and idioms picked up in various places during the Hutterite sojourn across Europe. In certain regions in Germany and Austria, such as the Tyrol or especially Carinthia, the Hutterite dialect can be understood even today.

Now numbering almost 50,000, we are in some ways a rootless people: severed from our homelands by persecution, Hutterites have had to make their home in many different places. Even our meals embody this history: the tradition of baking buns each Saturday morning surely has its origins in Germany. Hutterite *Worsch* soup, made of cabbage or beetroot, comes from the Ukrainian borscht. A Romanian teacher who taught at our school was delighted to find that our *Nuckela* was very similar to soup he had enjoyed back home.

Growing up, this was simply my world. I could comfortably exist and belong within it without experiencing any kind of division in my sense of self. It wasn't until my late teens that I became aware of how uncomfortably our established Hutterite culture sat with the radicalism of the Anabaptist pioneers. Like me, they had grown up within a tradition, an entire world of meaning and belonging saturated in its own rites, rituals, symbols, festivals and narrative structure. For me, this was Hutterianism; for them, it was medieval Catholicism. But then they heard the call: 'Come and follow me.' With that first baptism in Zurich, they stepped out of this matrix of belonging, beyond clan, tribe and family.

They hoped that by breaking with the institutional church, they could establish something closer to the perfection of the kingdom of God.

The Hutterite bishop Peter Riedemann wrote in 1542 describing the church of rebaptised believers as 'not having spot, blemish, wrinkle or any such thing, but pure and holy'.

Riedemann's words echo the apostle Paul's description of the church made perfect in the age to come (Eph 5:27). Though borrowing Paul's language, Riedemann uses it differently, applying it to the Christian fellowship here and now. But this amounts to an almost-fantastical claim, one that fits poorly with the all-too-human reality of the church at any point in time and certainly not the church in the present. Specifically, the Hutterite church of today hardly matches his description. Instead it stands as the lumbering legacy of its founders, stumbling through history, often unsure of its own reason for being, thwarting the cause of the kingdom it exists to promote. With its rigid traditionalism, internal divisions, self-absorption and growing materialism, it does not always seem an attractive body.

When considering baptism, I struggled with the prospect of joining a deeply flawed church. What did it mean to embrace the call of Jesus as my early forebears did, leaving behind home, family and land for the sake of the kingdom? How could I both claim the tradition of the community I loved and answer the radical call of the gospel? To find home, Jesus tells us, we must lose it.

THE BIBLICAL STORY turns on a 'stepping out' in answer to the call. The God who pulled the cosmos from the primordial *tohu wa-bohu* formed the people of Israel by calling a nomadic tribesman out of the land of his fathers. It is Abraham's response to this call from the unknown God that makes him the 'father of many

> As we are called out of our 'homeworlds' into the waters of baptism, so life in the kingdom of God calls us into foreign lands and friendships with unlikely people.

nations'. It is a tradition, a people, a story brought into being by the creative work of God. In the Gospels, God shows up as Jesus, the carpenter's son from Nazareth, summoning his disciples with the simple invitation, 'Follow me.'

In a sense, each person considering baptism must undergo this basic drama of stepping out of his or her 'homeworld' to follow the call into the life of the kingdom. The church is not a body of blood established by familial or cultural ties, but an eschatological community brought into being by the work of the Holy Spirit.

That's why anyone born into a particular Christian tradition must 'step out' of this belonging in order to truly belong. Only by returning to the vital origin of the tradition in the call 'come and follow me' can new life be breathed into dead bones. This is not a summons to become

first-century Galileans, or 16th-century radicals, but a call into the ongoing story of God's work in the time and place in which we find ourselves.

What, then, does it mean to become part of a broken church? Perhaps it means first recognising how my own hardheartedness, indifference and lack of courage contribute to the brokenness of Christ's body. And then recognising that the church is a body of broken people, gathered around the broken body of Christ, broken for us.

To be baptised requires faith in the creative work of the Spirit to make us what we are not. It is a faith that hopes there is more to the body of Christ than meets the eye. That there is more to the people who make up this body than their political views and faltering virtues. That the church's movement through history is propelled by more than economics, force and power, but is pushed onward by the breath of God.

THE HISTORY OF THE HUTTERITES is a story of contingency and surprise. At several decisive junctures in its history, the fragile movement could have been snuffed out. One of the most critical moments occurred around 1695, when the distinctive practice of communal sharing of goods was abandoned in Transylvania. After severe hardship and persecution from authorities, the Hutterite movement was on the verge of extinction.

But then came a surprise. In 1755, in an effort to suppress Protestantism in her domain, Empress Maria Theresa banished a group of Carinthian crypto-Protestants to the margins of her kingdom, forcing them to settle at Alvinz in Transylvania. This brought the Carinthians into contact with the demoralised Hutterites and the texts they had preserved. Inspired by their conversations and what they read in Hutterite homilies and confessions, the Carinthians joined the remaining Hutterites and established several communities, restoring the sharing of goods and giving the movement a second wind. My own ancestors, the Waldners, along with the Hofer, Kleinsasser, Glanzer and Wurtz family lines, joined the Hutterites from this Carinthian Revival.

If there is anything a peculiar people like the Hutterites ought to know, it is that we follow a surprising God – surprising not only in what he has done in coming to us in this man Jesus, but also in what he continues to do to carry this story forward. To follow this surprising God requires an attentiveness to what God might be saying and doing in the stuff of ordinary life, the present moment and the people, places and creatures around us. Such a life will be characterised by freedom, strange friendships and an openness to surprising possibilities. The ongoing renewal of the Hutterite tradition depends on our ability to hear and respond to this call. As we are called out of our homeworlds into the waters of baptism, so life in the kingdom of God calls us into foreign lands and friendships with unlikely people.

I, TOO, HAVE HEARD the call of this strange God. I stand as the last in a line of nine baptismal candidates. We have all grown up together. We are kin and blood. Now we stand waiting for the water. In unison, we recite the ancient creed of the church, 'I believe in God, the Father almighty, Creator of heaven and earth'. My mouth echoes the words that generations before me have spoken. I cannot pretend that my coming to these words was like reaching the conclusion of a syllogism. No doubt the formation I received from my parents, grandparents and community is a grace that precedes me. In the end, all I can say is that I find myself caught in the net of the kingdom of God.

'I believe in the Holy Spirit, the holy catholic church, the communion of saints, the forgiveness of sins, the resurrection of the body and the life everlasting. Amen.' I am claiming and being claimed by these words, being encircled by them and by the community that speaks them. We kneel and we pray for the Spirit of God to be among us. The water is poured. It runs through my hair, down my cheeks and to the floor. It comes dripping down to the light grey carpet, soaking it and turning it black like dried blood.

By Water

In a city astir with dangerous new ideas, the son of a priest becomes a leader of a non-violent revolution.

JASON LANDSEL

FIVE HUNDRED YEARS AGO, in an age marked by war, plague, inequality and religious coercion, there were people across Europe who dared to imagine a society of sharing, peace and freedom of conscience. These radicals were ready to die for their vision. They were executed by the thousands in both Catholic and Protestant states. *By Water* is a true story of friendship and betrayal set in the Swiss city of Zurich. It chronicles the conflict between establishment reformer Ulrich Zwingli (1484–1531) and his student Felix Manz (1498–1527), who at first reveres Zwingli as a father figure but ends up drowned on Zwingli's orders for insisting that only adult believers should be baptised. His fellow believers, called Anabaptists (rebaptisers) by their enemies, saw him as their first martyr. Facing intense persecution at the hands of both Catholic and Protestant authorities, the Anabaptists' courage and vision pioneered ideals that we still aspire to today: non-violence, economic justice, peaceful social reform and freedom of conscience.

Five years ago, I began seriously researching the story of Felix Manz and the Anabaptist movement he helped spark. I read dozens of books and travelled to locations in Europe including the street where Felix Manz lived, a cave where he may have hidden and the place where he was drowned. The title of *By Water* comes from an early Anabaptist text describing the punishments threatening anyone who was rebaptised: along with torture and loss of property both men and women faced execution 'by water, by fire or by sword'. All named characters in this book are historical figures, and the plot follows documentary sources, though some scenes have been imaginatively recreated.

Jason Landsel is a member of the Bruderhof and the co-author with Richard Mommsen and Sankha Banerjee of By Water, *a new graphic novel from which the following excerpt is taken.*

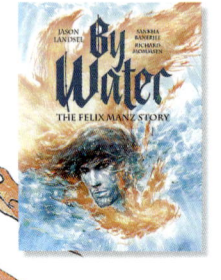

By Water
The Felix Manz Story

Jason Landsel and Richard Mommsen
Artwork by Sankha Banerjee

Softcover, 144 pages, £14.99 (see page 119 for subscriber discount)
21 March 2023

FELIX MANZ GREW UP
IN ZURICH.

LIKE ERASMUS,
HE WAS THE SON
OF A PRIEST.

SOME CALLED HIS
MOTHER A WHORE.

ZURICH WAS KNOWN MOSTLY FOR THE MERCENARY
SOLDIERS IT RENTED TO WHICHEVER POWER-HUNGRY
KING OR POPE WAS FIGHTING A WAR.

BATH HOUSE, WHERE THE SWEAT
ROOM IS A POPULAR SOCIAL SPOT

TAVERN, WHERE HARD-BITTEN
MERCENARIES GATHER

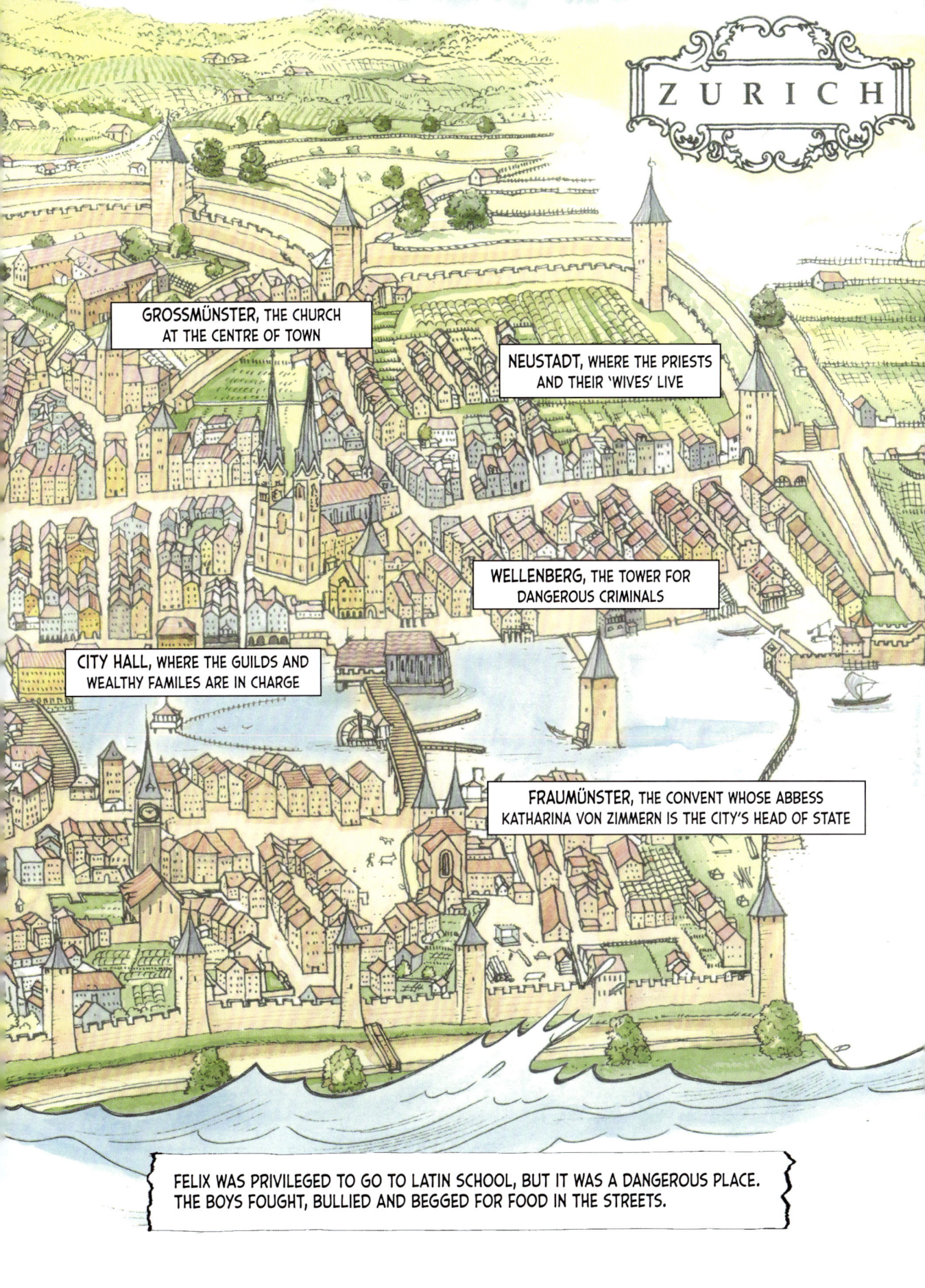

ZURICH

GROSSMÜNSTER, THE CHURCH AT THE CENTRE OF TOWN

NEUSTADT, WHERE THE PRIESTS AND THEIR 'WIVES' LIVE

WELLENBERG, THE TOWER FOR DANGEROUS CRIMINALS

CITY HALL, WHERE THE GUILDS AND WEALTHY FAMILES ARE IN CHARGE

FRAUMÜNSTER, THE CONVENT WHOSE ABBESS KATHARINA VON ZIMMERN IS THE CITY'S HEAD OF STATE

FELIX WAS PRIVILEGED TO GO TO LATIN SCHOOL, BUT IT WAS A DANGEROUS PLACE. THE BOYS FOUGHT, BULLIED AND BEGGED FOR FOOD IN THE STREETS.

MONEY FOR BLOOD!

WE ARE INVINCIBLE!

MAMA, I HAD TO FIGHT BACK. IT GETS WORSE IF YOU DON'T.

AGAIN? FELIX! A FIST, THEN A KNIFE, THEN WHAT? MURDER?

...AND WALKED 40 PACES UPHILL AND PRAYED BEFORE LYING DOWN IN DEATH.

WHERE THEY WERE BURIED, A CHURCH AROSE...

IT'S A MIRACLE! SAINTS!

...OUR OWN CHURCH, THE GROSSMÜNSTER OF ZURICH!

GROSSMÜNSTER!

A MIRACLE!

The story continues in the book By Water. ➤

Harper Henry, *Turquoise Traveler*, oil on canvas, 2019

NATHAN BEACOM

The Return of the Bison

In the Great Plains, scientists and small farmers bring back a mythic beast and a lost ecosystem.

THE PRIEST SAT READY to receive the sacrament, and the chief, with a long wooden spoon, fed it to him. It was not the Eucharist, but bison meat. Father Jacques Marquette's long Jesuit cloak was gathered about him on the Iowa soil. It was 1673, and he was the first European ever to come down the river. For the Peoria tribe of that time, feeding a visitor bison meat was indeed a sacred ritual – a sign of communion and welcome. This meeting was one of comity, though the encounters between European settlers and native people would, of course, be fraught and violent in the coming centuries. For now, with the sharing of bison meat and the calumet, there was friendship and peace. It was Father Marquette who first put down a description of the American bison in writing, calling it a 'wild ox'.

As this anecdote suggests, the bison has traditionally held a special place in the spirituality of the native people who have shared its ranges over the centuries. The animal was historically a font of life, a rich resource, a self-sacrificial creature that gave its last bone and sinew for human use. Food, clothing, tools, threads, needles, tipis – all manner of essentials were crafted from the bison's carcass. Later settlers also revered the bison, in their way: many civic buildings across the prairie states are adorned by bison as symbols of nobility and wisdom.

The American bison stands at the crossroads of the animal, plant and human worlds. It is part of an integrated ecosystem that includes people as much as it does bobcats, finches and sunflowers. Finding the right way to relate to this, our national mammal, might show the way to a healthy relationship with the natural world of the American West.

IT'S SEPTEMBER and the prairie is alive with the hum of pollinators. Yellow-flowered cup plants, wild bergamot and asters dapple the hills in gold, purple and white. The wind sends waves through the shoulder-high grass. I'm on an overlook at the Neal Smith National Wildlife Refuge outside of Prairie City, in Jasper County, Iowa. On the opposite hillside, a group of fuzzy brown balls are moving through the grass. These are the bison cows and calves. Much of the year, bulls are too rambunctious and there is a strict separation between the sexes. This is the time for mothers to nourish and raise their young.

'I like seeing the mothers and calves, they'll talk to each other. The mother will make her little noise and the calf will answer', says Karen Viste-Sparkman, the biologist on staff at the refuge.

'As you get to know them, you get to see they're individuals', she continues, recounting some favourite stories from her 15 years tending this prairie and its animals. 'There was one year that we had a cow that died after she had her calf. And I kept an eye on that one and kept in touch with the wildlife vet to know what we should do, how to tell if he wasn't going to make it.' Meanwhile, the calf had taken matters into his own hooves by 'going up to every adult bison, bulls included, and trying to nurse from them', she laughs. 'He ended

Nathan Beacom is a writer from Des Moines, Iowa. His work on agriculture and the environment and other subjects has appeared in Civil Eats, America Magazine, Front Porch Republic *and elsewhere.*

All artwork by Harper Henry. Used by permission.

up getting adopted by this yearling cow who had never had a calf of her own. It was just like mother and calf and they would stick together.'

Another pair that touched her had the care-taking going in the other direction, with a young calf looking out for an older cow. The mother was

see the buffalo wandering about thousands of acres of tallgrass prairie just south of Des Moines, Iowa.

The bison were an integral part of this first-ever major project in prairie restoration. This is true in two major ways, Viste-Sparkman tells me. First, in terms of the health of the prairie

---

> In the windswept remoteness of the prairie, huge sky overhead and interminable land all around, you meet face to face, the bison nodding and blinking slowly with its giant, thoughtful eyes, and there is no cloak of human civilisation about you.

---

three years old and went blind in one eye, and then the next year, blind in the other. She could no longer keep up with the herd on her own. But the calf ensured that his mother was never left behind, guiding and prompting her along.

This bison herd was brought here in 1996 to anchor the prairie restoration effort. Prior to settlement by Europeans, the state is thought to have been around 80% tallgrass prairie. Now, prairie is rare, with only 0.1% of the original prairie remaining.

In the 1920s, people began to notice that this landscape that once covered large regions of the American West had almost entirely disappeared. It clung only in the hard-to-farm places and along the railways. Aldo Leopold, the legendary conservationist, wrote in dismay in the 1940s about the future of the prairie and its largest resident: 'What a thousand acres of Silphium [compass plant] looked like when they tickled the bellies of the buffalo is a question never again to be answered and perhaps not even asked.' Incredibly, Leopold was wrong, and this points to the magnitude of the achievement of the Neal Smith refuge, for today, you may indeed

itself: the bison is a prodigious grazer, happy to munch on the bunchy, dry grasses of the Great Plains that are low in nutrition and indigestible by many other animals, as well as the richer grasses of the prairie. Its grazing habits enrich the diversity of the prairie, dispersing seeds across the landscape from its coat and scat and clearing space for new plants to come up and access water. Bison wallows, the muddy, wet sloughs it digs in summer, make an important resource for birds and breeding ground for insects. Bringing back the prairie has meant bringing back other species too. Henslow's sparrow, for instance, was almost non-existent in Iowa before prairie restoration picked up in the 1990s.

Illustration from the travel guidebook *The Great Northwest* by Henry Jacob Winser, 1883.

Harper Henry, *Good to Be King*, oil on canvas, 2021

Second, the bison is the finest ambassador for the grandeur of this ecosystem. 'The bison are here for the benefit of the prairie, but they're also here to educate', says Viste-Sparkman. Beautiful as the environs are, what people often *come* for is to see the bison.

From my own experience, in the more remote stretches of South Dakota, the encounter with a bison is a striking thing. In the windswept remoteness of the prairie, huge sky overhead and interminable land all around, you meet face to face, the bison nodding and blinking slowly with its giant, thoughtful eyes, and there is no cloak of human civilisation about you. And though the bison looks serene, if he should stand up and stamp, all the power of his massive frame becomes apparent.

The bison is enormous, its head larger than a man's torso. Its hair is 10 times thicker than domestic cattle's and that's not including the thick woolly undercoat. The bison has the lowest critical temperature of any bovine species, putting the yaks of Mongolia and the long-haired cattle of the Scottish Highlands to shame and is able to continue slowing its metabolic rate to survive efficiently at deep subzero temperatures. In these conditions, the bison body consumes energy at such a low rate that it can survive periods of intense cold and food deprivation. In the awful blizzards of the northern Great Plains, the bison settles face-first into the storm and trusts in the formidable insulation of its thick coat. But the bison is also fine in summer temperatures and, before widespread settlement, once roamed much of the interior of the continent, save for the deserts and coastal regions. Happy on sunny hillsides grazing rich grass, the bison will also use its massive head to shovel away snow and find forage in deepest winter.

WHEN IT COMES TIME for a rancher or a naturalist to work a herd of bison, the process is definitely a wilder one than with any domestic cattle. The bison panics if it is separated from the herd and it will buck and run like mad. But even as the bison retains its wild nature under human management, it is wrong to imagine these animals existing in pristine, untouched wilderness prior to the arrival of European settlers: bison were always in relationship with the people who inhabited this continent. Native peoples were managing herds (culling, guiding, using prescribed burns to direct them) for many centuries before Marquette came down the river.

But it's an old story how this balanced relationship was disrupted by Americans and Europeans coming west for economic opportunities: seeking gold, building railroads, revolutionising agriculture. The 'avarice of the white man', as US President Ulysses S Grant called it, meant that he was constantly making incursions on native lands and this led to violence. Perhaps most famously, gold mining in the Black Hills of the Great Plains led the United States to shirk its treaty obligations to the Lakota people, which in turn led to the bloody conflict of Little Bighorn and what followed.

Leaders in the United States Army, like the legendary Civil War generals William T Sherman and Philip Sheridan, undertook to clear away the American Indians from emerging American settlements and railway lines, confining them to designated reservations. But so long as the buffalo roamed across the west, native hunters would follow. Forcing out the American Indians, therefore, required clearing the bison so central to their way of life.

The Army encouraged hunters to travel west and bag as many buffalo as they could. At the time, it seemed as though the animals were endless. It is thought that their number in the American West exceeded 30m. But a herd of buffalo out in the middle of the prairie was no match for hunters with long-distance rifles, and by the end of the 19th century, they were almost extinct. Private industry was even more responsible than the Army for this collapse. In the middle of the century there was a brisk trade in bison hides. So unlike native peoples, who used the whole buffalo, hasty hunters would skin the animal out on the plains and leave the carcass to rot. Hides flooded the market and the trade in bison eventually cratered, but not until the creature had been overhunted nearly to the point of no return. Even the cowboy William 'Buffalo Bill' Cody, who purported to have killed more than 4,000 bison in just eighteen months, was writing in dismay by the end of his life about the damage that he and hunters like him had done.

Ecologically, the loss of the bison coincided with the loss of the prairie. Humanly, it coincided with the near loss of native cultures and ways of life, contributing to generations of economic and social disadvantage for those growing up on Great Plains reservations. As the bison went, so went the West.

'TO PROTECT THESE ANIMALS, we have to use them. They have to have a purpose or they will go extinct', Gail Griffin tells me, of the movement to raise bison for meat. 'Buffalo go through the thread of this country for thousands of years, and if we don't protect the species, we lose something.'

Thirty years ago, when Gail and her husband, David, moved into a rundown old farm, they never imagined it would become the business it is today, Rockie Hill Bison. 'When we first got here, the place was basically unlivable', Gail says from across her sturdy kitchen table. 'When we drove in to look at the place, I just told her "Don't look at the house"', David laughs. He's a big man in overalls and white goatee with a face that looks stern

'The person we bought it from farmed up and down the hills. Corn and beans. Nothing else. We put in strips and waterways and got it cleaned up.' Fortunately, David used to own an excavating company and had the machines to move all of the detritus from the land and start to bring it back to health. Without that, it would've been too expensive to rent those machines and get it cleaned up, the couple agrees.

Ultimately, restoring the health of this farmland was tied to putting bison back on it. But that wasn't the original inspiration for getting the animals. 'There was a guy who owned a concrete company in Winona. He came up to me one day and he said, "Every contractor has got to own some buffalo." I looked at him and said "Sure."'

Ultimately, restoring the health of this farmland was tied to putting bison back on it. But that wasn't the original inspiration for getting the animals.

---

until a chuckle or a good story lights a twinkle in his eye. We're on the eastern border of Minnesota, near the city of Winona, on those beautiful bluffs that line this stretch of country along the Mississippi. It's February and sunny but well below zero. The cold, clear light sparkles off the snow, and, in the distance, bison huff soft clouds of steam, not looking the least bit cold.

'You should've seen it. The basement was full of junk. We opened a shower curtain down there and it was just hundreds and hundreds of shampoo and detergent bottles and so much junk down there', Gail says. David adds, 'And the outside was just like that too. This guy had actually had people pay him to dump their junk in the ravines on the property, so there were just piles of old appliances, refrigerators, washer machines, other junk. Took about two months to make it livable inside.'

As the prior landowner had approached his own home and waterways, so also had he approached his soil, that was degraded and full of chemicals.

David makes a sceptical face. '"Why? You got some?" And he said, "Yeah I won 'em off some guys in a game of poker in Iowa." He had them out by Highway 61 just north of town and said, "Come on, I'll show you some." I looked at them and bought three calves right there.' Back in the 1990s, apparently, there was quite a boom in buffalo hobbyists. David was hooked, and just needed to convince Gail (who would go on to serve as president of the National Bison Association). Up to then, they'd been feeding young bull calves for David's dad, but it was too time-consuming, whereas bison are low-maintenance. David and Gail only work their animals once a year.

Over time their herd grew and they had to develop what had been a nearly non-existent market for their meat. Today, they send their animals for processing at a local plant and sell them to supermarkets and restaurants. They also sell to the local school system and Gail, who has a background as a hospital nutritionist,

Harper Henry, *American Bison*, oil on canvas, 2018

teaches the school kids about healthy eating and local livestock agriculture. In the 1990s, though, wealthy people just wanted animals and had no plan for what to do with them. I ask the couple if bison ranching had been consistently growing since they started. The answer is yes and no. Around 2000, with all these growing hobby herds and inexperienced ranchers and no market built for meat, bison ownership crashed. Producers had to get serious about marketing their product and finding ways to get it out in front of people. 'We were serving chicken at our own National Bison conferences', remembers David. In the years since, the bison meat market has grown tremendously and, with it, the number of herds of bison that roam hills much like these.

Bison are a fitting meat for our day, when consumers and producers alike are more aware of the ill effects for the environment and animal welfare of conventional livestock agriculture. Many customers also appreciate how nutritious and lean bison meat is. A typical meat cow is fattened on maize at a centralised feedlot before heading to one of the factories of the Big Four American meat companies for slaughter, and a typical hog may spend nearly its whole life in an indoor pen. The concentrated animal waste these industrial farms produce is bad for waterways and, with them, there is no longer the reciprocal ecological relationship between the animal, the plant life and the soil. Bison, by contrast, roam free, feeding on a complex mix of native grasses.

At the same time, the ongoing existence of these animals, at least at scale, depends in part on their agricultural production. 'You can't afford to have them just because, or because they're good for the environment', Gail says. 'You've got to promote the meat to promote the animal.'

Along the way, 'it's caused us to do a lot of research on what was here before, and we've added more than 87 native plant species to our pasture now', she continues. 'We've spent time learning about what was on this land. We've become grass farmers who happen to harvest that grass with bison.' I ask the Griffins what inspired them to take a piece of land that was sick and spend nearly 30 years bringing it back to health. 'It was a challenge', David winks. 'I'm kind of bullheaded.' In meeting this challenge, they have taken a piece of land with degraded soil, serious erosion, low diversity and a heap of rubbish and turned it into a flourishing ecosystem. With the bison and the grass back, the insects are back, the topsoil is returning and the birds too. 'When we first moved here, in 1993, The National Audubon

We step outside into the frigid Minnesota weather to look at the bulls. As we walk, some of them look away and some square themselves at us and paw at the dirt. Even in the dead of winter, this hill country is beautiful, and I can see the trees Gail and David have planted lining the ridges and valleys. Looking into the big, obsidian eyes of a bull, I think on how it was a handful of bison calves that brought all this – this interconnected revival of animal, plant and human community – about.

THE LAKOTA SAY 'Mitákuye Oyás'iŋ' – that we are all related, that the tallgrass and the buffalo are part of our extended family and we of theirs. Human beings need not be foreigners in nature, unless we act wrongly. If we act as if the rest of the world were only raw

---

Our teacher the bison shows us a way of relating to the natural world of which we are a part, a world where each part is connected and all things are held in balance.

Society came out and counted 26 bird species; they came back about ten years ago and counted 97', Gail says. 'We have sandhill cranes here now. All of a sudden you'll see a new bird show up. Tanagers. I'd never seen a tanager, and over in our east woods there's a fairly good population. So I get my small thrills here', Gail laughs.

They are collaborating with their neighbours to restore the land. One landowner alone can't control invasive species or chemical pollution. 'It forces you to talk to each other, rather than just say, "Ugh, look what they're doing over there"', Gail says. 'We are known for working together and learning together.' The project is intergenerational: 'Our grandson has been into bison since he was a little kid, and now he's 19 and wants to take up after his grandparents.' Gail looks ahead to what their efforts will have yielded 50 or 100 years from now. 'These will be things that will carry forward when we're gone.'

material for our human desires, we corrupt and abuse natural balances and laws that we did not create and cannot really change. But if we treat the natural world's own forms, patterns and laws with respect – even when we are using it to support human needs – we might be relatives.

This is what the Griffins are doing, and what the Plains Indian reservations are doing with their revived bison herds. We can find ways to reap the resources we need from the land while also being its caretakers, keeping in mind the beauty and worth of a place beyond just its profitability.

Our teacher the bison shows us a way of relating to the natural world of which we are a part, a world where each part is connected and all things are held in balance. This ancient ambassador for our continent reminds us of our tie to, and responsibility for, the particular land on which we live. We need the bison, and the bison need us.

On Planting Sugar Maples

How do you pass on a legacy, and how do you receive one?

DAVID JOHNSON

'A good man leaves an inheritance for his children's children'. —Proverbs 13:22

O N A RECENT VISIT to my childhood home, I walked under trees I had planted as a teenager. What were once spindly maple saplings dug out of the woods and transplanted with hope of future maple syrup production are now 30-foot trees. The copper beech, given to us by a neighbour in exchange for planting one for him, is now 40 feet tall and providing summer shade. The wild azaleas, dug out of the western Pennsylvania woods to plant in our cemetery, now bloom near the graves of dozens of my childhood mentors.

My lifelong love for gardening and horticulture began when my parents, Howard and Marion Johnson, started us on a family garden that we kids tended with Dad's advice. (He had exhausted his desire for land work during the Great Depression, with countless childhood hours spent chopping cotton, followed by years of large-scale farming in southwestern Georgia where he grew peanuts, maize, sweet potatoes and forage crops.) And as I remember my parents, I can't help considering their improbable journey up from the Bible Belt South, a journey both geographical and spiritual.

My parents did not leave me a material legacy, but rather something much more valuable: a life lived in service to Jesus, sharing in full community of goods and welcoming all others seeking to live out the kingdom of God in the here and now. They did not pressure or persuade me to do the same, but their example of devotion to their brothers and sisters ultimately proved irresistible.

Dad and Mum began their life in Christian community at Koinonia Farm in Americus, Georgia, right after their wedding in 1949. They then moved to the Bruderhof in 1956. Because we left Koinonia when I was four, my memories are few: playing with Tippy, my beloved puppy; gashing my leg jumping off a corrugated iron table; watching Florence Jordan cut off the head of a rattlesnake.

But all my life, my parents told us about the

David Johnson is a pastor in the Bruderhof communities in the United States. He and his wife live at the Fox Hill community in New York.

protests in Washington, DC and brought home literature that exposed our military's intervention in Southeast Asia for what it was. He counselled numerous young men on how to become conscientious objectors, an act of repentance for his role as a navigator of a B-29 Superfortress in World War II, in which he flew multiple bombing missions over Japan.

The 1965 civil rights march from Selma to Montgomery that Dad joined became a highlight in his memory. Knowing the risks, he told me before he left that he might not come back alive and asked me, age 13, to be ready to care for my mother and siblings.

I, too, wanted a life dedicated to the fight for racial justice and against war and dreamed of joining the turbulent social revolutions of the 1960s. The community I grew up in did not do enough, I felt, to actively combat the ills of society.

Koinonia venture with its gospel-based stand against racism and war, lived out in the context of Christian community. They could not say enough about Clarence Jordan, Koinonia's visionary founder and how his witness drew them out of their Bible-Belt inheritance of racism, patriotism and the dream of upward mobility. My father often spoke of his visit to Martin Luther King Jr's home in Montgomery, Alabama, shortly after it was bombed in 1956. Stopping in unannounced, Dad was welcomed in by Dr King to spend the evening. His connection to Koinonia was enough to gain the family's trust and friendship.

As I grew older, I began to understand what my parents' radical decision to follow Christ cost them. Ostracised by their relatives for their opposition to segregation, they found their once-promising careers cut off by their decision for a life of voluntary poverty at Koinonia, where their days were filled with unrelenting work. Yet they never spoke a word of complaint about any of it.

Later, in the 1960s, Dad – a World War II veteran turned pacifist – participated in anti-Vietnam War

A T THE SAME TIME as I was absorbing the witness of my parents, I began to work with Alfred Gneiting, the community's gardener, who years later would become my father-in-law. Alfred was born in Germany, with a childhood shadowed by the Great War and a soul longing for some way to respond. Rebelling against the Marxist socialism of his stepfather, Alfred had first participated in the YMCA, which at that time had a strong evangelistic focus. Drawn by the German Youth Movement, he joined a free-flowing band of youths who travelled the countryside, seeking a deeper connection to nature and an escape from the status quo, from organised religion to political intrigue to class divisions. Eventually, at the age of 20, he found his way to Sannerz, the first Bruderhof community, in 1924. Here his ideals could get to work.

Seeing my interest in planting trees, Alfred drafted me to help him with his landscaping work, a job I kept through my secondary school years. From Alfred I learned to plant trees the 'correct' way: his way. He demanded absolute

Top, Howard Johnson *(far right)* working at Koinonia Farm;
bottom, Howard Johnson's photograph of the 1965 march from Selma to Montgomery.

adherence to his instructions. We spent hours wheeling barrows of topsoil and compost to our projects, often up a steep hill. Because of his emphysema, Alfred would pause frequently to catch his breath.

During these pauses he would tell me about his elation at finding a life of brotherly community. He recounted one anecdote after the other about Eberhard Arnold, whose understanding love, warmth and clarity drew out the best in Alfred and the other strong-willed individualists whom God had assembled to build up a life based on the early Christian way. Thus I absorbed the legacy of the early years of the Bruderhof community and of Arnold's prophetic voice. Though my sense of unbelonging persisted, seeds were sown that would take root and blossom later.

After finishing secondary school in 1969, I set off to make my mark on the world, filled with the confident assurance that I was ready for anything. While proud of my parents' work in building a radical alternative to the American Dream and deeply influenced by Alfred's example, I did not have a personal faith in God or belief in Jesus Christ. Before I could embrace and own my legacy, God had to break down my self-assurance so that I could recognise my own sinfulness and seek the peace and healing of Christ in my own life. As a friend once told me, 'God has no grandchildren. He only has children!'

Back home on a visit from college just days before my 18th birthday, I attended a church service that included a reading from Eberhard Arnold: 'The Great Objective'. It reiterated concepts that I had heard repeatedly ever since I could remember. However, on that Sunday, 12 October 1969, my heart finally opened to their message:

> The kingdom of God is in the future, but its effect extends into the present...This is a justice that takes practical shape as economic and social brotherhood among men; a peace that means we live in peace with each other and can have nothing to do with war, violence or lawsuits; a joy that

> means that what we do is ruled by love for others and joy in them...The real evidence of the Holy Spirit's action is unity and community in daily work and life, harmonious sharing of production, consumption, labour, leisure, grief, joy, aims, actions and all of life. If this unity is missing, it is better not to do so much singing, praying and preaching...Trusting faith can already see the whole earth flooded in light with the dawning of God's kingdom...This is what we are to live for, and in the strength of grace, can live for. There is work to do!

Hearing those words, it dawned on me with unforgettable clarity that God was calling me to live for his kingdom in full community of goods with these particular brothers and sisters. The legacy of Alfred and of my parents now became mine: they were the good men of the proverb who had 'left an inheritance for their children's children'. I finally understood that everything I'd dreamed of finding had been right in front of me the whole time.

Fifty-three years later, it's my turn to speak with young men and women of the upcoming generation who are asking the eternal questions – what can I give my life to? How can I make it count? When I look up at the tall trees that Alfred and I planted together or the wild azaleas that now bloom near his grave, when I see how far their roots have extended into the good soil and towards each other, it occurs to me that it is much the same work. ⤫

Top, Howard and Marion Johnson; *bottom,* Alfred Gneiting.

PLOUGH BOOKLIST

The Problem of Pain

The God Who Heals
Words of Hope for a Time of Sickness
Johann Christoph Blumhardt, Christoph Friedrich Blumhardt

These 60 short daily reflections, each based on a verse from the Bible, will help guide a believer facing serious sickness to trust in the will of God. With confidence in the healing power of God and the possibility of miracles, the Blumhardts, a father–son team of pastors, point us away from our troubles and towards a Creator who wants the best for each of us.

Rick Warren: Whatever circumstance you are facing right now, this book of daily readings will help you focus on a closer relationship with Jesus, our one true spiritual healer. Soak in these words of hope by the Blumhardts and find healing strength for your soul.

Hardcover, 208 pages, £12.99 £9.09 with subscriber discount

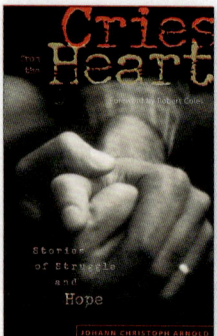

Cries from the Heart
Stories of Struggle and Hope
Johann Christoph Arnold

In times of crisis, all of us reach for someone or something, greater than ourselves. For many, it can feel like talking to a wall. People are looking for assurance that someone hears them when they cry out in their despair, loneliness or frustration. Instead of theorising or preaching, Arnold tells stories of real men and women dealing with adversity. Their difficulties range from extreme to quite ordinary and universal; readers will see themselves in these glimpses of anguish, triumph and peace.

Softcover, 226 pages, £8.99 £6.29 with subscriber discount

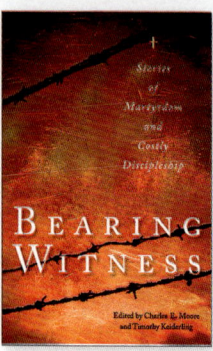

Bearing Witness
Stories of Martyrdom and Costly Discipleship
Edited by Charles E Moore and Timothy Keiderling

Stories of the boldness and steadfastness of early Christian martyrs have been handed down from one generation to the next. But the stories of more recent Christian witnesses are often unknown, even within their own faith communities. This book brings together dozens of accounts from around the world of believers who gave witness to Christ in the face of intense persecution, reminding us what costly discipleship looks like in any age.

Softcover, 242 pages, £9.99 £6.99 with subscriber discount

New Releases

By Water
The Felix Manz Story

Jason Landsel, Sankha Banerjee and Richard Mommsen

This historically accurate account of young people standing up for their convictions against the corrupt political and religious leaders of their day will appeal to today's non-conformists. This graphic novel is the first in a series that dramatically recreates a little-known chapter in the history of the Reformation.

A true story of friendship and betrayal, *By Water* recounts the conflict between establishment reformer Ulrich Zwingli and his student Felix Manz, who ends up drowned on Zwingli's orders for insisting that the state should not dictate religion. In this visualisation of the birth of the Radical Reformation, water is both wonder and weapon, a symbol of new life and a death sentence. See an excerpt from the book on page 92.

Kirkus Reviews: An ambitious biography – in graphic-novel style – of an early Anabaptist martyr. Intriguing watercolours – evocative of both Hieronymus Bosch and 1970s pop art – precede the opening pages...The chapters that follow use accessible language and abundant visual cues in softly coloured, action-packed art.

Softcover, 144 pages, ~~£14.99~~ £10.49 with subscriber discount

A History of the Island
A Novel

Eugene Vodolazkin

Translated by Lisa C Hayden

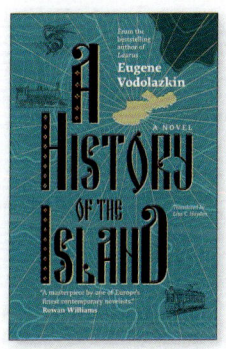

Monks devious and devout – and an age-defying royal pair – chronicle the history of their fictional island in this witty critique of Western civilisation and the idea of history itself.

Eugene Vodolazkin, internationally acclaimed novelist and scholar of medieval literature, returns with a satirical parable about European history, the myth of progress and the futility of war. The chroniclers dutifully narrate events they witness: quests for power, betrayals, civil wars, plagues, droughts, invasions and revolutions. But at least one monk simultaneously drafts and hides a 'true' history, to be discovered centuries later. Vodolazkin recasts history in all its hubris and horror, while finding the humour in its absurdity. For readers with an appetite for more than a rational view of what motivates, divides and unites people, *A History of the Island* conjures a world still suffused with mystical powers.

Rowan Williams: Compelling reading: brilliantly vivid and inventive, it combines magical–realist mischief with a compassionate, radically Christian perspective on the self-destroying idiocies of human history and political posturing. A masterpiece by one of Europe's finest contemporary novelists.

Hardcover, 320 pages, ~~£19.99~~ £13.99 with subscriber discount

The Communion of Empty Hands

EDUARDO GALEANO

Though he was an atheist, the Uruguayan writer Eduardo Galeano (1940–2015) knew several pastors and lay Christians who were imprisoned by his country's authoritarian government in the 1970s and '80s. This story is based on their accounts.

NINETEEN SEVENTY-THREE. Montevideo, Ninth Cavalry barracks. A rotten night. Roar of trucks and machine-gun fire, prisoners facedown on the floor, hands behind their heads, a gun at every back, shouts, kicks, rifle blows, threats...

In the morning, one of the prisoners who hadn't yet lost track of the calendar recalled, 'Today is Easter Sunday.'

Gatherings were not allowed.

But they pulled it off. In the middle of the yard, they came together.

The non-Christians helped. Several of them kept an eye on the barred gates and an ear out for the guards' footsteps. Others walked about, forming a human ring around the celebrants.

Miguel Brun whispered a few words. He evoked the resurrection of Jesus, which promised redemption for all captives. Jesus had been persecuted, jailed, tormented and murdered, but one Sunday, a Sunday like this one, he made the walls creak and crumble so there would be freedom in every prison and company in every solitude.

The prisoners had nothing. No bread, no wine, not even cups. It was a communion of empty hands.

Miguel made an offering to the one who had offered himself. 'Eat', he whispered. 'This is his body.'

And the Christians raised their hands to their lips and ate the invisible bread.

'Drink. This is his blood.'

And they raised the non-existent cup and drank the invisible wine.

Source: *Voices of Time: A Life in Stories*. Copyright 2006 by Eduardo Galeano. Translation copyright 2006 by Mark Fried. Published by Metropolitan Books, an imprint of Henry Holt. By permission of Susan Bergholz Literary Services, Lamy, NM, USA. All rights reserved.